HOW TO CHEAT LIKE A MAN

HOW TO CHEAT LIKE A MAN

A How-To-Guide for Women Who Want to Stray, Play and Get Away With It

PAULO ROSSI

Dedication

To all the beautiful women of the world

Table of Contents

GOLDEN RULE
#3

GOLDEN RULE
#4

GOLDEN RULE
#5

GOLDEN RULE
#6

GOLDEN RULE
#7

GOLDEN RULE
#8

GOLDEN RULE
#9

Introduction

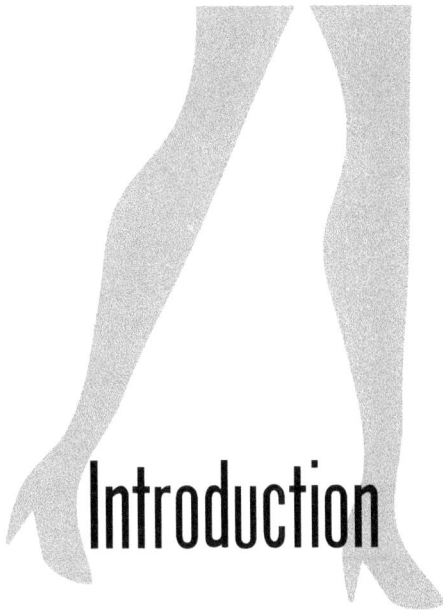

Okay, ladies, so you think because your husband or boyfriend never notices when you get a haircut or wear a new dress that he won't notice if you're having an affair?

Think again!

While we men may be oblivious most of the time (each season has its own sport, you know, and they're not going to watch themselves), we are very perceptive when it comes to certain things. Such as any other guy touching our woman. Or our car. Or our golf clubs. Though not necessarily in that order.

That's why, if you're a woman of any age who's either married or in a serious relationship—and want to *stay* that way—you need to have a guide if you're going to have an affair. *This* guide: *How to Cheat Like a Man*.

However, although this book was written by a man primarily for women, anybody in a relationship, such as a college student, a gay man with a boyfriend, a married lesbian, a mature woman with a companion, and, yes, even a married man, can benefit from the teachings and techniques in this book. But back to my girls…

So what makes this guide so unique, you ask? Because there isn't any other one like it. It's a practical, step-by-step guide for women (or, as we've seen above, almost anybody!) on how to cheat successfully, and it was written by a man. It will show you how men think, what signs men look for, what makes us suspicious, and which common mistakes to avoid.

What this book shares with you are **The 9 Golden Rules**—the necessary measures that every woman must follow if she wants to cheat on her companion but is determined to stay in her marriage or relationship at any cost. It also explains the consequences if she doesn't follow them.

You may be wondering why a guy is writing a how-to guide on cheating for girls. Well, for one thing, there's no better way to know what makes a man suspect his woman of having an affair than to hear it from a man—and asking your significant other is obviously out of the question. Calling your father or brother is a bit creepy, and waiting for Dr. Phil to cover the topic on his talk show is a crapshoot. So, honestly, I'm by far your best shot.

For another thing, men don't usually need a guide on how to cheat. Most of us are hardwired to cheat, though not very successfully. We tend to be a little too cocky to listen to any advice. That's why, after a supposed "business meeting," many of us think a few layers of bad cologne is enough to cover up the smell of strippers (it can't; stripper scent is industrial strength). Then, when we finally stumble home, we wonder why our wives/girlfriends won't talk to/have sex with us and have contacted a lawyer/a moving van/a sexual addiction rehab center for us.

Women, on the other hand, are more methodical about most things. I don't mean manipulative or conniving by that (though you ladies certainly know who you are!). I just mean that women plan and are always prepared. Kind of like Boy Scouts. Only with breasts. And without those khaki uniforms. (To any woman reading this now who may happen to be wearing a khaki uniform, first, please accept my sincere apologies. Second, you might want to put this book down for the time being and pick up a fashion magazine before deciding to try your luck at a fling. Trust me on this.)

In short, women will exercise caution, use prudence, take the helpful advice presented in these pages, follow The 9 Golden Rules and be able to cheat successfully and keep their relationships (and reputations) intact. Men, on the other hand, will continue to bang their babysitters and secretaries and then brag about it and get caught.

There is yet another overriding reason I am writing this manual. For the record, I am not advocating cheating by any means, but the fact is that it actually happens all the time. Whether or not I approve. No, I am not trying to capitalize on infidelity. That is for the divorce lawyers and owners of "no-tell motels." What I am actually trying to do with the effective and proven The 9 Golden Rules is to help marriages/relationships and minimize any collateral damage.

Finding out that a partner is cheating can be pretty tough to handle to say the least. Emotions run high. Self-esteem takes a hit. Attorneys are called. Families are torn apart. And all for what? Because one woman decides that she is not getting what she needs from the relationship (most likely after trying to address the issues time and again to no avail) and takes action. To me, that doesn't seem fair. Infidelity does not mean that a person is ready to give up on a marriage/relationship. In fact, sometimes, quite the opposite. That person is trying to *protect* the marriage/relationship. Hence, there is a need to conceal the affair and keep the person's partner in the dark. For his own sake and the sake of your relationship, it is the right thing to do. The purpose of The 9

Golden Rules, then, is to protect what is most valuable—to you (your relationship) *and* to your man (his ego).

In fact, many have argued that, with infidelity, everybody wins. The woman is getting the attention and romance she deserves. Her man gets a happier partner with a renewed spring in her step—*without* having to do any extra work. And the "other man," well, we all know what he's getting.

The infidelity ends, the marriage/relationship continues, there's lots of great "guilt" sex (no worries, ladies—we men will happily take whatever we can get...besides, we won't know the source of your rekindled passion; we'll probably just assume that our two-day growth and wrinkled T-shirt make us irresistible to you in a macho, unkempt kind of way— don't be surprised if we don't shave or do laundry for several days thereafter), no feelings are hurt, and the best part is that nobody's the wiser. As they say in old bank robbery movies, "We get in, we get out, and no one gets hurt."

Of course, that scenario works only if you follow **The 9 Golden Rules** presented in this book. Otherwise, infidelity can mean complete disaster.

Now there are some people who might argue against infidelity no matter what and may not see the practicality and plus side to this how-to guide. They may even object to the fact that it's the woman who's doing the cheating. After all, aren't women the pillars of virtue in society? The bastions of self-control and self-denial? The cheated-on, who stand by their man, rather than the cheaters, who have another man on standby?

To that I say, "Yeah, sure they are." And they buy the Massaging Touch finger vibrator only to work out those kinks in their necks from cooking over a hot stove all day.

We are in the second decade of the twenty-first century. It is a post-feminist world in which most equal rights have already been achieved. Oprah is the most powerful person on the planet, women are literally in the driver's seat even when it comes to NASCAR, and a transgendered man has actually had a baby. Isn't it time we realized that wives and mothers (or potential wives and mothers) are women—and people—too?

And despite what we see on sitcoms, women actually enjoy sex—and some will go out and have affairs when they aren't completely satisfied in their relationships. Men don't have a monopoly on that, you know.

Let's face it. When a man has a fling, no one is really that surprised. Unless the number of mistresses reaches into the double digits, there's nothing too shocking about the realization that men are highly sexual beings who will go searching for sex like pigs go looking for truffles. If we feel we are not getting enough, we will step out of our homes, turn over every rock, and go rooting in the dirt until we find it. Why should we be surprised that women want the same thing?

According to a report done in February 2009, 45 to 55 percent of women are cheating on their partners, compared to 55 to 60 percent of men. That's not a big margin of difference. To extend our metaphor, women can be pigs just as well as men.

It is an old cliché that women are imbued with beauty and virtue and men with lust. Okay...it's a cliché that holds some truth. Women are beautiful, and men can't seem to get enough of them. And because of that, most women have their pick of men more or less. So why would they stick to just one?

It is my belief that most men will cheat when the opportunity presents itself (I'll leave the physiological, psychological and theoretical discussions about why this occurs to professionals in other fields). But why do women cheat? All the reasons we hear for men having affairs ("There wasn't enough sex," "She didn't seem interested in me anymore," "I didn't feel appreciated," "Did I mention there wasn't enough sex?") apply just as much for women. Plus there are plenty of other considerations for having a fling:

☞ Is it to feel more attractive or desirable?

☞ Is it to boost your ego?

☞ Is it to feel young again?

Or, since all of the above can be satisfied with a visit to the plastic surgeon's office, is it to find something that's temporarily missing from your current relationship or your life?

Obviously, the motive for cheating varies from one woman to another. But there is essentially nothing wrong with going after something you want or need at the moment, provided it doesn't do damage in the long run or harm someone you truly love. Cheating shouldn't change how you feel about your partner. Think of it like a mini-vacation to Barbados: it's a great place to visit, but would you really want to live there and be doing all that waxing every other day? Pretty soon you'd want to put down the margarita, pry the thong from out of your butt, put on some sweats and curl up on your comfortable but decidedly less glamorous couch in front of the TV. Think of the other man as a beach in Barbados and your man as that soft, slightly worn-in sofa. When you've had enough of the heat, you'll be dying to get on him again.

The benefits of cheating, like a good vacation, are that it can make you feel refreshed, reinvigorated and more alive— but the best part is that it can make you appreciate even more what you already have waiting for you at home.

Before sociologists, religious pundits and marriage counselors everywhere—not to mention my grateful readers—begin sending me thank-you notes, fruit baskets, Nobel prizes and nude photos (you can find my address in the Yellow Pages) for my work in saving the institution of marriage and relationships in America, they may want to ask one thing: what makes me such an expert?

Since no institute of higher learning actually gives out certificates for cheating, I can't really cite any diplomas or advanced degrees in that department. But what I can tell you is that I am an engineer, which means my mind works systematically and without emotions, which is something you want if you're carrying out programs—or planning an affair. I believe in eliminating risks or reducing them to an absolute minimum in all matters. I spent months designing and formulating The 9 Golden Rules and then, through ten years of practical usage, I tested, refined and perfected these guidelines. I'm by no means bragging about my accomplishments (successful affairs), nor would I put it on my resume, but I do have long-term experience in cheating successfully. This is who I am.

A few years ago, on a Sunday afternoon, as I sat at a golf club restaurant having lunch with two of my closest friends, Samantha and Jennifer (their names have been changed to conceal their true identities), the subject of cheating came up in our conversation (and I'm not talking about cheating on your golf score, though those two were definitely doing some of that as well—and don't think I didn't see them!). For the first time, I confessed my past infidelities, which spanned a ten-year period while I was in steady relationships with different girlfriends back in New York. My friends were at once astonished and impressed when they discovered what I had been up to for all those years. Then they became upset and angry—not that I had cheated on my girlfriends but that I hadn't shared with them the secrets of my success sooner.

Samantha and Jennifer admitted that they never suspected me of being the cheating type—especially with so many different women and having gone undetected for so long. The reason they never suspected anything was because I was so attentive, thoughtful and affectionate toward my girlfriends the whole time. We seemed to have the perfect relationships, which, in a way, we did, and they never—to this date—discovered my infidelities.

I disclosed to Sam and Jen that part of my success was due to the fact that even they—two of my closest friends—were unaware of my infidelities and the secrets that I never shared with anyone. But they demanded access to these classified techniques and the training that I used so well to conceal my affairs for all those years. I agreed with their request, did a quick sex-change on The 9 Golden Rules with emphasis on what makes men suspicious of their wives or partners, and the teaching began.

Modifying The 9 Golden Rules to apply to women was actually pretty easy, considering my expertise and background. Knowing what I know about cheating, I approached it from a male perspective: What would I be looking for to see if my wife was fooling around? What would be the telltale signs of infidelity in a woman?

Shortly afterward, Sam and Jen both got married eight months apart. Sam used The 9 Golden Rules detailed in this book and applied them religiously (um, make that "rigorously") when she committed her infidelities, whereas Jen got cocky, ignored the rules and paid the price for her affairs. Jen has been through four divorces so far; Sam is still happily married to her first husband.

While it is true that for ten years, my girlfriends were utterly unaware of my interest in other female companions and the intimate relations that I had with them, by no means is that a guarantee that the methods, techniques and training described in the following chapters will be 100 percent successful for you. However, if employed and adhered to, The 9 Golden Rules will substantially increase your probability of success more than any other approach—except maybe abstinence. And we all know how well that works. Just ask anyone in high school. Or in the clergy.

If you are considering engaging in infidelity, know that is an art form that requires dedication, discipline and (ironically) commitment. It is not prescribed or advocated for all, just for those who have enough courage and tenacity to go after what they want while protecting those they love. In short, most women.

It is not my place—nor anyone else's—to pass judgment. We are not living in some 1950s "women's weepie" or melodrama in which the woman who strays has to live with the shame and stigma of her actions. We are talking about a fling, a flirtation, fun!

To that end, however, you must be fully committed to your endeavor and to success in your affair. It is not all fun and games. Too much is at stake for that. Treat it as an undertaking that requires a cool head, a calm heart and a commitment to your goals (i.e., not having your relationship or family structure crumble). Most important, it takes sufficient strength to walk away before getting too emotionally attached.

Cheating does not mean that you are a bad person, or in the majority of cases that you're any less in love with your man. It means that you're a woman with needs, wants and desires. It means that you're human.

When done right, infidelity is not a sign of weakness or "giving in" to lust. Far from it. Planning your encounters, organizing your affairs and setting the limits are all signs of strength, *not* weakness, and they put you firmly in control.

A man has the illusion that when he meets a woman and it leads to a short-lived intimacy, the action is to be considered his achievement. In reality, it is the woman who chose him and allowed the connection to be consummated. Remember: women always control sexual situations; without their consent and desire, no encounter would ever transpire.

However, you can't control everything—and that's where having **The 9 Golden Rules** firmly in place can save the situation, not to mention your relationship should things take an unexpected turn.

The uncanny part about cheating is that almost the minute you commit infidelity, it appears that your partner immediately becomes suspicious. Maybe you're acting guilty, or your body language is somehow giving you away; maybe he's not suspicious at all, but your conscience is tricking you into thinking he is. My recommendation is to trust yourself and stick with the plan. Read this book carefully and methodically from beginning to end. Mentally absorb as much as you can of what you read, making notes in the margins or marking certain paragraphs or sections that you may need to refer to later on.

Of course, the unwritten rule is that no one can find out that you're reading this book. Some of you, I'm sure, ordered it online, knowing your husband never bothers to get the mail, or you had it delivered as a signed-for package to your office. Others picked it up in a bookstore—hopefully one *way* out of town—and perhaps mentioned to the store clerk, "It's for my sister-in-law" (if you don't get along with her, you may have even casually dropped her name). Where you are hiding it heaven only knows. It may be in your purse, near your "feminine products," at the bottom of the laundry pile or somewhere else we men fear to go.

You, dear readers, have already shown great promise. You know that while cheating is meant to be fun and lighthearted, it is also serious business that should not be undertaken lightly.

Most of you know that a committed relationship is worth saving—even if that takes some lying on your part—and that the man you're sleeping with on the side would be a lot less attractive if you had to see him scratching himself in his boxers every morning and spitting toothpaste in the sink before bed every night. The point is that you know the difference between fantasy and reality. You know what's real and what's temporary. You know what you're willing to live with and what you're not willing to lose.

Remember, cheating can be nothing more than a little harmless fun. As long as you play by the rules—The 9 Golden Rules.

·

#1

Always Plan Ahead

To master the art of infidelity, you must first adopt a custom of setting goals, organizing your thoughts and preparing a set of instructions to achieve them. This process is commonly referred to as "planning"—and women are usually experts at it. They plan outfits to wear, vacations, weddings, parties and all sorts of other events. So why should an adulterous affair be any different?

No step leading to an act of infidelity should be without thorough planning. The absence of this tool will most likely result in the destruction of your life and lifestyle as you know it. There can be no mistakes made when so much is at stake. You know what you want. Now you must make a plan to go out and get it.

Having a fling should not be a spur-of-the-moment thing. Forget romance novels and French movies. No one here is getting her bodice ripped atop a pile of hay or running off with a stranger on the train after smoking a few packs of cigarettes and discussing existential philosophy. This is not fantasy or film. This is real life, with things to take into account such as divorce, custody battles and estranged emotions. (Okay, that last one can also be found in French movies, but you get the point.) For your purposes of cheating on your man and getting away with it, you have to be methodical and strategic. That may not sound very romantic, right? But it's the difference between keeping your *head* and not losing your *heart*.

The first step you have to take in this process is admitting to yourself that you are feeling bored of, tired of, ignored by, dissatisfied with or just plain fed up with your husband or boyfriend and you're missing that tender, loving touch of a man to bring excitement, joy and sexual intimacy back into your life.

This initial step is essential. It is not about judging yourself. It is about facing the eventuality. If you are honest with yourself and have confessed that cheating is not an "if" but a "when" proposition, then you will be prepared to act accordingly when the time comes. Otherwise, who knows? One look, one smile or a particular type of cologne could just be enough to derail your life in ways you never thought possible. Getting swept off your feet is not all that it's cracked up to be. You could easily land on your ass. Make a plan, and be prepared to carry it out.

Planning reduces risk and limits the possibility for mistakes. Just as important, planning helps to remove emotions. A woman who commits infidelity must act a bit like a robot or a dead fish (not hard for some of you I've met) so that emotions and feelings do not interfere with her decisions or plans. Planning in advance helps to reduce unexpected emotions, and it also assists you in focusing and maintaining order and self-discipline in your affairs.

As we will see in the second *Golden Rule*, getting emotionally close to the other man is extremely risky—and a woman, especially one thirty or older—will sometimes develop feelings for a sexual partner rather quickly. Planning will help to prevent that. Of course, no plan is bulletproof or without flaws; however, not having one is even worse because it increases the likelihood of failure.

The effectiveness of a plan is in the details, and following the details as outlined in your plan is crucial to getting away with cheating on your man. What separates a good strategy from a bad one is the attention to detail that goes into its design—the "how to," step-by-step process. The "how-to" phase is the one during which you do the most thinking, analyzing, risk assessment and risk mitigation; the one during which you pay attention to the smallest details to ensure maximum success.

When the details are being worked out, always assume that the worst can and will happen to you. Your thought process should get realistic and systematic—nothing should ever be left to chance. When you plan for a goal, you are forced to analyze each step, especially if you draw out the plans on paper, which also encourages execution. A written plan could constitute evidence against you; therefore, you must hide it in a secure location and discard it as soon as your short-lived affair has ended.

Planning puts you in charge of your affairs and in control of the events happening around you. Once, when I was just twenty-six, early in my career, I had the chance to meet a self-made multimillionaire in his villa in Spain. As I talked with the impressive seventy-nine-year-old man, I mentioned that I would like to know his secret.

He replied, "Secret? There is no secret. I'll gladly share with you anything I know...but I will allow you to ask me only one question."

I knew this was my one chance. I thought long and hard about it and then asked, "Can you share with me the most important fundamental, basic methodology you employed, regardless of the endeavor, that has made the biggest contribution to your success?"

The multimillionaire nodded, apparently impressed with my thoughtfulness. As I lifted my pen and pad, preparing to take notes, the gentleman smiled and said just one word: "Planning."

Finances and infidelity are two areas in which you want to leave nothing to chance. Plan it out—or pay the price.

You should always plan according to the level of risk. No one walks down the street and suddenly gives in to an impulse to rob a bank or commit a jewelry heist; any self-respecting robber first develops a well-thought-out and detailed plan. The same planning principle should apply when you consider cheating on your spouse or companion since the emotional and financial consequences could be enormous.

However, you need to understand that no matter how well you draft your plan, it is utterly meaningless unless you actually use it to steer your actions in the right direction, toward your ultimate goal. That's why you need to plan each step—from *before* the beginning to the eventual conclusion.

How to Choose Your Target

Once you've admitted to yourself what you have in mind, the next most important step is choosing an appropriate target. You should have a general idea in mind of the man you're going to sleep with *before* you even meet him. This is where it can get tricky.

You know that guy at work—the one with whom you flirt without meaning to, the one who gets your jokes *and* gets you coffee? You've started thinking of him as your office husband and comparing him to the real thing. When the two of you have worked late together a few times, you didn't even mind not getting paid overtime. He's the one who might have gotten you started thinking about how you're dissatisfied with your own relationship. You know the guy I'm talking about?

Well, he's not the one.

Not for our purposes anyway. The problem is you're already too close. This would not be some quick, passionate fling. This would be a full-blown love affair. And who the hell needs that? Such affairs are time-consuming and emotionally draining. If you are missing drama in your life, buy theater tickets. If you are missing fun, excitement and sexual passion, pass this guy up.

For men, I would recommend a one-night stand with a stranger. For some women, I could see how that might be unseemly. For others it could be hot, depending on your point of view and your view of porn. However, for married women, the one-night stand with a stranger may be the best bet because there are no ties between you, and all is forgotten the next morning. These flings are also optimal for women away on business trips.

If you're not into one-night stands, you might want to try the middle ground: not someone you *know* exactly, but someone you've seen around. He should know nothing about you and live nowhere near your home. That way you won't run into him with your husband or boyfriend—and you'll have no trouble walking away.

So what does this guy look like? The attributes of a perfect "partner in crime" include:

☞ Someone subdued who doesn't look like he needs to brag to his friends about his "conquests." (Flashy gold chains are a warning sign!)

☞ Someone relatively nondescript so that if anyone sees you together you can always say, "That was my brother [or cousin]. Didn't you recognize him? Brown hair, medium build, average height?" Sorry, ladies, that means no George Clooney or NBA players—and no public displays of affection, for obvious reasons (i.e., incest).

☞ No one who looks too lonely or seems too desperate. You may have the strength to walk away, but do you really want to be bothered with getting a restraining order or having him drop by your house. (Remember the boiled bunnies in *Fatal Attraction?*)

☞ No prison tattoos. On the one hand, due to the high rate of recidivism, chances are good that he'll end up back in the joint before you have to break it off. But on the other hand, getting involved with him could be more trouble than it's worth (i.e., what starts as a fling could land you in Sing-Sing).

This selection process may seem to limit you a little, but it also offers up a variety of questions and choices. For instance,

Would you rather have a young cub or a silver fox? Some women prefer breaking in a young one because they're malleable, grateful and—let's face it—filled up and ready to go every fifteen minutes, sort of like a shuttle bus from the airport. Others, however, would rather skip the training session and go with experience. As long as the cub can keep his mouth shut, you're good either way.

Would you rather he be married/committed or single? The former seems like a safe bet since he has as much at stake as you do, but some women may sympathize too much with his wife or girlfriend—and we're looking for a good ride, not a guilt trip here. A single guy would be a good choice as a sexual partner so long as he isn't too clingy or too much of a player. What woman wants to feed into that?

If you can't find the right guy, you can always consider hitting for the other team and find a willing woman for some hot lesbian action. (Come on, ladies…I'm a guy! You knew I had to try at least once.)

It is important to consider these questions carefully and plan on selecting an appropriate target with whom to have an encounter—otherwise it's quite possible that an urge or a powerful sexual attraction will cause you to be unfaithful when you least expect it…with exactly the wrong type of man.

Where to Find Your Target

Think about possible guys (or girls…we want to keep an open mind here) who fit the profile and who you've seen around someplace where your significant other doesn't tend to go: your gym (a good choice since he'll probably be fit), a department store (another good choice since he'll probably be well dressed), or a coffee shop near your office (that's hit or miss, depending on how you feel about over-caffeinated sex). Your target should also not be situated near your home or your husband/boyfriend's office. In fact, ideally, your target wouldn't live anywhere near you, which is why they invented business trips in the first place. (We'll discuss more about this idea later under the "69 rule.")

Some "cons" to consider are that the potential target shouldn't know anyone else you know—and you should be prepared to look for a different gym, department store or coffee shop after you've had your fun. That might mean having to give up a really good café au lait for a really good lay. Your choice.

The "pro" about finding someone in such "regular" surroundings is that it would seem to indicate that he's a regular, normal, stable guy and not some psychopathic lunatic. Always a plus. Bookstores and grocery stores are also good for that sort of thing as opposed to, say, a therapist's waiting room or outside a free clinic.

Of course, bars and clubs will do the trick, too, but be prepared to go in by yourself since, as I've written in the introduction, not even your closest friends or family members should know about this excursion. That means you'll be a woman alone in a room full of horny and half-drunk guys. Perhaps that's the perfect setting to find a man...but in some cases it could be closer to a feeding frenzy.

If you find yourself in such a place, choose your target wisely. Avoid the ones who look like "regulars" because they'll surely blab to the bartender—and anyone else who'll listen. Steer clear of the creeps, of course, and stay away from those who've had too much to drink or your one-night stand might not be able to "stand at attention" when it really counts.

In a place where men are ripe for the picking, remember to go in with a basic game plan of the type of man you're looking for. Don't just pick up the first guy who gets your attention after the third tequila. Stay sober and stay selective.

Keep in mind the list from the previous section on "How to Find Your Target" and try not to stray from it all that much. That will cut down on the potential for regrets due to impaired judgment or an impending last call. Remember, it's all about planning, not impulse. So if the right guy isn't there that night, you can always go back.

Invent Another Identity

Knowing your target is key, but who says he has to know too much about you? Let's face it, ladies. Men are not all that picky. Or discriminating. Or attentive. We don't have to know your life story to want to leave with you—we just have to know that you're alive and willing. So to protect your identity and your relationship, don't give away more than you need to.

What I'm doing here is letting you women in on something that we men have been doing for quite some time: inventing false identities. You know that guy you hooked up with before your current relationship—the one who never called back? His name wasn't really Manny Banister. And he wasn't a lawyer, a Wall Street broker, a heart surgeon, an NFL player or whatever else he told you he was. What he definitely was, though, was married or in a relationship. He just invented an alternate identity: a means to an end.

And now it's your turn.

Even if you're out of town or in a pitch-black bar where nobody knows you, you're going to want to try to keep your real identity to yourself as much as possible. In other words, go into this with *true* intentions but a *fake* name!

The last thing you want is your one-night stand or temporary fling to find you on Facebook and try to "friend" you or to look up your name on LinkedIn.com and show up at your office.

(In fact, before the affair occurs, it's a good idea to remove your photos from all online networking sites altogether.)

Come up with an alias well in advance—something sexy, like "Ingrid" or "Natasha," is good, but such names may work better if you're a tall blonde rather than, say, of Chinese descent. Similarly, "Ming" or "Ebony" might not fly for a fine redheaded Irish lass. Keep it real—even though you're faking it—and be certain to add a last name or he'll know for *sure* you're hiding something.

It may be best to select a common first name but a surname that is unusual, uncommon and hard to pronounce. It should be difficult to remember, repeat and spell, and it should hardly resemble your actual last name at all. (I recommend using Google to search for a German, Polish, Greek or otherwise tongue-twisting ethnic last name; out of politeness, he probably won't ask you to repeat yourself more than twice.) But make sure you choose a name that's memorable—if only to you, that is!

As for your choice of careers, don't try to pass yourself off as an airplane pilot if you can't even drive a stick shift. If you tell him you're a fourth-grade teacher, know which subjects that should entail and have a school name in mind (avoid using "South Park Elementary" or "Springfield Elementary"; any self-respecting guy with a TV set and opposable thumbs to work the remote will know you got those from *South Park* or *The Simpsons*). Again, the more detailed planning you do ahead of time, the more realistic your new identity will sound, and the less you'll give away about your true self and situation.

Sure, you can choose a profession that has a good chance of impressing the gentlemen, but do *not* get carried away. Your new career should be one that you know something about. At the very least, do some research on the Internet to acquaint yourself with your chosen profession and learn some buzzwords to be convincing.

As for your hometown, place of birth and schools, make sure they are far away from your current residence, the place you were born, the place you're visiting and where you *actually* attended high school and college. However, you must have some familiarity with the selected towns (and schools). Details *matter*. Pick somewhere you visited a few times in the past and know your way around—but where nobody knows you.

If all else fails, use the Internet to find a town, high school and college of your choice, and then learn everything you need to know online; just make sure you know enough to carry a conversation. Familiarize yourself with two sites in case your target happens to be from one of your selected towns. To avoid an awkward moment, always take initiative when you meet your target to discover where he was born, has lived and all other pertinent information about his past and present.

When it comes to your friends, create some imaginary names and occupations. Have some fun with them! Make them as interesting and influential as you want them to be. This technique is not only great for conversation material but it also derails the attention from you and puts it on the friends who do not exist.

If your target asks you the places you visit for your job (which usually comes up in small talk, especially when you're on a business trip), generate a list of towns that you have visited, but make sure that they are far from places where you actually go for business or spend time with your family.

Even when you're out of town, the less you talk about yourself, the less chance there is that something will slip. If you feel you're getting in over your head, always be ready to change the topic of conversation as quickly as possible and redirect it onto him. For example, you could say things like, "Enough about me. I want to know more about *you*." "Where did you say you went to college?" or "So tell me about this town. It's my first time here." This diversion technique works well on all men but especially well on younger men; they will always prefer to speak about themselves and their lives than to hear about yours.

Despite how challenging and time-consuming it might sound to come up with a whole new identity, in order to elude detection you must take no chances and leave no trace behind when you leave. Familiarize yourself thoroughly with all the elements of your new identity until they are etched in your brain and are, in fact, a part of you.

Don't feel bad about "lying" or making things up. Men do it *all the time*. This is a fling, not the start of a serious relationship. Fun and flirtation are factors here—honesty and openness are not. Remember: the truth will set you free—as in being a "free agent" once your supposedly "one-night" stand calls you at home a few days later and your significant other dumps you immediately. Keep your personal information personal.

Details Are Essential

What finding a target, faking your identity and playing a role all have in common is close attention to detail. You need to plan the time for your tryst, plan to find the target, plan an alibi, plan an alias... A "one-night" stand is made up of "a hundred and one" details.

In fact, it has been said that the most essential element for success in any part of life is planning. We plan when we want to purchase a home, buy a new car, go on vacation or organize a birthday party—all down to the smallest detail. Doesn't it make sense to do the same when we want to commit infidelity with so much at stake?

Planning is an ongoing process, which means your plan

will need to be updated frequently in order to meet new challenges or unexpected obstacles as intention becomes action. It may be only a one-night stand, but it takes a lot more than one night to figure out the details and to plan for any potential fallout.

Cheating is an act, a goal—and getting away with it is an achievement that requires detailed planning if you are a woman already involved in a relationship. You simply cannot undertake such an act without careful forethought because the consequences could be life-altering.

Therefore, before you begin, you should think out and plan each part of the infidelity so that the entire process goes exactly the way you want it to (which is, of course, the bottom line here). That's why this is the most important first step you can possibly take to ensure a satisfying fling.

Effective, detailed planning will help you to recognize personal strengths and potential opportunities of which you can take advantage in order to increase your chance of a successful liaison. (For example, if you know you're going away on a business trip or your significant other will be out of town, that's the time to put your plan into action.)

Proper planning also helps you to see way ahead of time any weaknesses in your strategy since you will revisit and revise the details as many times as needed; this will allow you to remedy those weaknesses before the plan is carried out (for instance, coming up with a viable excuse for an amount of time for which you cannot account).

Planning lets you keep focus, saves you time and energy and enables you to concentrate on the most important goal—committing adultery and getting away with it—with the *least* amount of fallout and the *most* amount of fun.

Finally, planning assists you in organizing your thoughts and in identifying all the key issues that must be dealt with in advance to eliminate potential risks that might expose your affair. If a stain on a dress could get a president impeached and almost thrown out of office, coming home with your panties turned inside-out could surely turn your relationship upside-down.

Okay, so planning all the details in advance might not seem like the sexiest thing in the world. But I guarantee you that it will make the whole situation work out more smoothly by taking away a lot of the worry and allowing you to enjoy yourself that much more—which, after all, is the whole point of having a fling! Spontaneity may sound more exciting and adventurous, but it leaves a lot more room for things to go drastically wrong, which is about as un-sexy as it can get.

Think of it like this: wouldn't you rather plan to go skydiving and bring along a parachute than suddenly decide to jump out of a plane and hope for the best? Sure, both ways may be "so far, so good" the whole way down. But the difference is in how you land…and I'm here to make sure you land on your feet!

Case Study #1

In light of what we've learned from *Golden Rule #1*, let's consider the cases of my close friends Jennifer and Samantha to convince you of the importance of planning ahead:

Let's go back in time to when Jen was still married to her first husband, Rob. One night, she decided to have a drink with a few of her friends from work at a bar nearby their office.

One hour and several drinks later, Jen noticed a good-looking young guy at the bar staring in her direction and smiling. She'd been feeling a lack of affection from Rob lately because he was focused on his work, and so she was enticed by the attraction, especially after listening to her single friends' stories about their recent conquests with men. Soon enough, her hormones won out over her better judgment, and without any thought of the consequences she left her table and approached the bar, where the man immediately bought her a drink.

They started talking, joking and laughing with no regard for appearances or the fear that someone from work might see her flirting with a total stranger and spread it as gossip. A couple of hours later, her colleagues left the bar, but Jen stayed behind.

Shortly afterward, the guy invited Jen to his place, which was only about ten miles away from her house. Flattered (and a bit buzzed), she accepted the offer, figuring that Rob would be working late anyway. Besides, she was excited by the prospect of an affair and a little attention.

Jen drove to his apartment complex, parked on the street and followed him upstairs. Along the way they stopped on the stairwell and exchanged a few passionate kisses, seemingly unable to keep their hands off each other or wait long enough to get inside the apartment.

Once inside, Jen looked around while the guy poured them each another drink. She knew it was an expensive address and thought that her new friend seemed a little young and not quite well off enough to be able to afford the two-bedroom apartment.

But she never bothered to ask if he had a roommate or lived alone.

He brought the drinks over to the sofa, where they relaxed a while before getting caught up in a more heated exchange.

Suddenly, with her shirt half off, Jen heard a bedroom door open, and who was standing there but Mike, an associate of Rob's?

"Jen?" he asked, clearly surprised. "What's going on? Rob didn't tell me you two split up."

"We didn't," she muttered, trying to cover herself the best she could.

She was caught in the act and could only apologize and leave immediately with the hope that Mike would have enough mercy on her not to mention the incident to her husband. It turned out that she was lucky that time. Mike kept silent, and the rumors going around her office never made it back to Rob, fortunately.

Let's review our model, keeping in mind that planning provides guidelines to help you make good decisions. In this example, Jen had no plan or preparations and, as a result, made a few poor decisions:

- ☞ There were too many witnesses to her indiscretion, including coworkers, neighbors in the apartment complex and anyone recognizing her car outside.

- ☞ She went back to his apartment, which was too close to her home, her office and her husband's place of work.

- ☞ She did not ask enough questions of her potential one-night stand beforehand to find out about his living situation.

The fact that he was a young cub should have tipped her off that he wasn't the right target.

In all of these areas, proper planning would have identified the risks and guided her to avoid such an embarrassing and potentially damaging situation altogether. Literally as well as figuratively, she could have lost her shirt.

Now let's compare that scenario to a better-planned strategy. A couple of years ago, Samantha was working late into the evening on a lucrative proposal with representatives of a venture capital firm. One of the accountants she was working with was handsome and charming, and she noticed an undeniable attraction. After everyone else had left, he and Sam took a break and started talking about life and their personal interests. They soon discovered that they had some common hobbies and even knew some of the same people in the industry.

When they left for the night, he suggested that they go out and get a drink. After all their hard work, they certainly deserved it. Sam was tempted but thought about it for a second and gracefully rejected his offer. They shook hands and parted ways.

Amazingly, here was this good-looking, intelligent, interesting man asking her to go for a drink—and maybe more than some fun flirtation—but her answer was no. Why did Sam reject his offer when she was definitely entertaining the idea of infidelity? The answer is actually quite simple: she had not planned for this opportunity to materialize, which meant that she did not have time to carefully analyze the consequences of her actions, nor had she made any step-by-step preparations following The 9 Golden Rules.

By then, Sam had had a few successful encounters outside her marriage and was able to see this unexpected opportunity as a possible source of entrapment—something she wanted to avoid at all costs. She demonstrated self-control and good strategy by walking away from the man and the potential damage he could present to her relationship.

Importantly, Sam had quickly analyzed the risks, which were:

☞ The man already knew her name and place of business, which meant he could contact her well after their "one-night" stand was over.

☞ She asked enough questions to get to know her target and determine that both of them knew many of the same people, meaning the news of their tryst could easily make its way around the same circles that she and her husband traveled in.

☞ Any bar where they went for a drink would be too close to her workplace and home, which increased the odds of her being spotted and would have eliminated any possible alibi of her staying late at the office.

Yes, both women had a similar goal, but only Sam had a strategy. While Jen's lack of planning could have cost her her marriage—not to mention her reputation at work—Sam's attention to detail and her determination to stick to the plan saved her and her husband potential pain and embarrassment. She may not have sealed the deal with the joint venture capitalist that night, but by putting the same plan into action a short time later with a more appropriate target, she was able to enjoy a very successful merger.

GOLDEN RULE

#2

Keep the "Love" out of "Love Affair"

Think of Golden Rule #2 as the cardinal rule—follow it and you will get exactly what you want out of an affair: an ego boost, attention, choice, fun, freedom, flirtation…and you will avoid all the things you don't want: commitment, hassle, jealousy, drama...in short, another relationship. But by all means, ladies, to achieve this you have to learn to keep emotions out of it!

A very wise woman with very long legs once posed the philosophical question, "What's Love Got to Do With It?" The answer: absolutely nothing. If you're looking for love, you may want to glance over at the guy next to you on the couch later. Even though he may not be much to look at right then, sitting in his boxers and elbow-deep in a bag of chips, he's the real deal. What you're looking for in an affair is sex, pure and simple. (Okay, maybe not so pure...but definitely simple and with no strings attached.)

Men seem to have no problem with the "no falling in love" rule whatsoever. We don't have to love a woman to want to bang her; conversely, once we bang her, we don't confuse the feelings of lust with love. Emotions don't even enter the equation—except perhaps gratitude.

Now I'm not saying that women are more emotional than men, so don't cry, yell, eat a tub of ice cream or whatever it is you ladies do when you're having feelings. I'm just saying that we men keep our emotions separate from each other in the same way a dog humping someone's leg doesn't suddenly develop feelings for the leg or the person it's attached to. How do we do that? "Emotional immaturity" you say? Well, we call it "self-discipline."

Self-Discipline

Developing self-discipline is paramount in implementing your plan and achieving your goal of cheating on your significant other and getting away with it.

Being disciplined means behaving according to what you have already decided is the best thing for you regardless of how you may feel at a given moment. Developing a detailed plan (as discussed in the previous chapter) is a great way to practice discipline—so long as you stick to it. Otherwise it's an exercise in futility. You have to know yourself and trust yourself to follow the plan that you laid out. It's what successful soldiers do in the heat of battle and what successful adulterers do in a heated embrace. If the plan was to be long gone before breakfast, you shouldn't find yourself sharing pancakes and coffee with the new guy come morning. Hit the road at midnight (or whatever time your plan calls for) and head to an all-night IHOP if you're hungry. Just don't let yourself get lulled by the sweetness of the moment or deviate at all from the original plan. If you get careless, you get caught!

It all comes down to acting according to what you *think* instead of how you *feel* in the moment. If you realize that falling in love with someone else will jeopardize your relationship with your significant other, then it's simple: just don't fall! Self-discipline often involves sacrificing an immediate pleasure or thrill for what matters most in life.

Keep in mind that for each of us—no exceptions—emotion will affect our judgment and force us to *react* instead of acting accordingly, thinking things through and following the designated plan. This is the reason *Golden Rule #1* tells you to plan things in advance. Planning gives you the strategy and self-discipline to follow through on your intentions so you won't get blindsided by the power of the emotion. A simple formula is: planning = empowerment...emotions = a loss of discipline.

How to Develop Self-Discipline
(Otherwise Known as "Easier Said Than Done!")

It's nice to think that we all have a degree of self-discipline. But anyone who's ever been to Vegas, text-begged an ex-lover to return or drank 'til they puked (sometimes all three in one night) can attest to the fact that self-discipline does not always kick in when we need it most. All those embarrassing, pink-eyed, inebriated pictures you see posted on Facebook or MySpace are evidence of this.

The not-so-nice truth is that self-discipline takes training. You have to train yourself to accomplish certain tasks or practice particular patterns of behavior—including keeping your emotions in check—even though you might really rather give in to what you want at the moment. It's true for finishing a marathon, staying on a diet or successfully carrying off a one-night stand. So don't fool yourself into thinking you're the exception to this rule and that you don't need to practice self-discipline. Everyone does, especially when it comes to infidelity. It's the difference between simply getting tangled up in the sheets or getting into an emotional entanglement.

So how do we develop self-discipline? Let me be the Mr. Miyagi to your Karate Kid. Sorry, ladies…I mean the Tim Gunn to your *Project Runway* contestant. To make this work, we have to practice.

Okay, young grasshoppers, the first exercise we're going to do involves an impartial self-examination to determine how disciplined you are and what you must do to improve this area.

In a daily planner or on your computer, make a flow chart (see example, Shawn's Birthday Party) and select an overriding goal for the top box, such as throwing a big, elaborate birthday party for your significant other (that will also help you score points and offset suspicion).

In the smaller boxes below, write the general steps necessary to accomplish the goal.

Below these general boxes, fill in additional sub-boxes with details and each necessary step required to accomplish the more general steps.

Once the plan is developed, set it aside for two days and perform additional brainstorming and research on how to accomplish your goal, adding complexity, texture, nuance and detail. For example:

Shawn's Birthday Party				
Guest List	Select Location	Develop Menu	Select Dinks (Wine List)	Send Invitations

Set Aside Plan for Two Days	Review & Refine Plan as Needed	Set Aside Plan for Two Days	Do a Virtual Walk Through	When Satisfied Put it into Action

Review and refine the plan as needed.

Again, set it aside for another two days and perform additional brainstorming/research a second time; add some twists (for example, if you were planning an outdoor barbecue, come up with a second plan for if it rains).

In your mind, do a virtual walkthrough of your plan, taking everything into consideration—including what could go wrong; refine it as needed.

  ☞ Carry the daily planner or flow chart with you when performing each step that you have detailed in your plan.

  ☞ Check each step as you perform it to see your progress.

☞ Perform all the steps you set out in your plan without any exceptions until the goal has been reached to satisfaction.

Allocate about one week for this exercise and, upon completion, evaluate the result. The important items to consider for your self-examination should be:

☞ Did you accomplish your goal?

☞ Did you reach your goal in the allotted time?

☞ Did you make necessary alterations or revisions where appropriate?

☞ Did you deviate from the plan or skip any steps once it was in motion?

If your response to any of these questions is no, then you are lacking the required self-discipline to see your goal through and should not embark on an affair at this time until you practice and improve your self-discipline. Believe me, you'll be doing yourself (and your significant other) a favor. But don't despair; even if you're very undisciplined now, you can use this exercise to build it up. The more disciplined you become, the easier it becomes to accomplish your goals. Pretty soon, carrying on a successful adulterous affair will seem like child's play.

The second exercise is even less fun. But trust me—you'll thank me later!

Again it involves a daily planner.

Keep it in your BlackBerry, on a calendar or in a journal—it doesn't matter. The important part is to fill it with things you absolutely *don't* want to do—and then do them all! That teaches you how to stick to a plan and keep your emotions or spur-of-the-moment whims out of it.

Also, be sure to include long-term goals that you have to build on (like we learned in the first exercise) as well as short-term goals.

The chart on the following pages provides an example.

Notes

_____

_____

_____

_____

_____

_____

_____

_____

_____

_____

_____

_____

_____

_____

Sample of a Weekly Plan

Monday	Tuesday	Wednesday
Exercise @ gym 6:30-8:00 am	Exercise @ gym 6:30-8:00 am	Update 401K plan before work
8:30 am—Handle your least favorite tasks/clients at work first	8:30 am—Handle your least favorite tasks/clients at work first	8:30 am—Handle your least favorite tasks/clients at work first
Review Stocks @ 5:30 pm	Review insurance policies @ 5:30 pm	Pay bills/update banking @ 5:30 pm
Dentist 6:30 pm	Make phone calls that you've been dreading	Doctor check-up 6:30 pm
Shop for and cook an elaborate dinner (no shortcuts)	Do office work before bed	Shop for and cook an elaborate dinner (no shortcuts)
Sex with significant other (kidding!)		Clean dishes/kitchen right after dinner

Thursday	Friday	Saturday	Sunday
Exercise @ gym 6:30-8:00 am	Take a cold shower (winter)/ hot shower (summer)	Go for an early morning jog	Wake up early
Be the one to make the coffee, fix the printer, clean your desk	8:30 am— Handle your least favorite tasks/clients at work first	Clean out closet	Read your least favorite section of the newspaper first from cover to cover
Take your car for 25K service directly after work	Go to dinner with acquaintances or relatives whom you've been putting off	Do various household chores or improvements	Clean out the garage
Inheritance planning	Come home and work or workout instead of relaxing	Visit Mom/ Dad or in-laws	
Watch part of a movie you enjoy; force yourself to walk away halfway through		Plan holiday/ birthday gathering in detail	Plan tasks for next week

The advantages of this kind of exercise are numerous. Being goal-oriented and detailed reduces the chance of risk and failure; it also keeps your mind focused on the completion of your task, not allowing time for your thoughts to wander or to create diversions for yourself.

Remember, you cannot cheat on your boyfriend or husband unless you have a plan, possess self-discipline and have the will power to see it through from beginning to end, even if there are other things you'd like to do or additional time you want to spend with your chosen target. If you become disciplined enough to accomplish your goals in a given timeframe, this ability keeps your behavior planned and predictable, causing fewer chances for mistakes or unexpected emotional entanglements.

You Don't Have to Stand by Your Man
(But It Would Be Nice if You Could Still Stand Him)

Compartmentalizing is another key to keeping the "love" out of "love affair." You have to train yourself—which, again, takes discipline—to separate your extracurricular activities from your real life. When you're with your boyfriend or husband, *be* with him. Don't be reminiscing about last night's sexcapades or distractedly dreaming about your next target. No one needs that kind of threesome!

As last section's exercises showed us, there is a time and place for everything. Your affairs are planned out—they have a time limit and a definite expiration date that you must obey, even when it comes to training your own mind to focus on the moment at hand. Letting your thoughts stray to your one-night stand when you're at home with your loved one is like inviting the other guy in to have dinner with the two of you. You have to keep him—and all thoughts of him—in his place and in proper perspective...and that takes *tons* of self-discipline.

Engaging in an affair is a lot more serious than having a schoolgirl crush. (Not that I've ever had one myself...) If you find that your affairs are infringing on or detracting from your day-to-day life with the one you love, it may be time to take a break from the infidelity for a while and refocus your attention on your real relationship or exactly what it is you want.

It's also essential not to make comparisons between your significant other and your one-night stand. Why? Because your man will always come up short—and I'm not just talking inches. Sex with someone new is usually going to be thrilling and exciting (or at the very least awkward and, well, exciting), whereas sex with someone with whom you've been for a while is guaranteed to get old. That doesn't mean the new guy is better in bed and you should start thinking about trading up; it just means the novelty factor hasn't worn off yet. However, in a few months' time (if you were to allow the affair to go on that long, which you won't), the sparks would gradually fade. That's why one-night stands and strict time limits for affairs are optimal in the first place. The thrill is still there, but the guy is gone.

It's also important to know that the other man—no matter how amazing he may seem for a night or two—has the same bad habits and imperfections as your significant other. You just don't have to stick around to see them. If you find yourself idealizing or romanticizing the new guy, picture him doing the same disgusting things your boyfriend or husband does on a daily basis. You're welcome...oh, and welcome back to reality.

Falling in love with your target isn't the best outcome of your infidelity—it is without a doubt the worst, especially if you want to keep your relationship with your significant other. Of course, not all women are created equal; some (bless their little hearts) do not develop emotions or feelings when engaged in sexual activity with someone other than their partner. They are the lucky ones; for them, the fear of falling out of love with their partners does not exist. It isn't even an option. They simply do not allow themselves to get trapped in a love triangle.

If you are not one of the lucky ones, then you have no choice but to trick yourself and your emotions by altering your mind-set. It's a bit of self-deception rather than self-discipline and is considered one of the best practices to avoid falling in love or becoming infatuated with another person when you are being unfaithful. In fact, this technique is often used by medical school students whose desire for sex is no different than the rest of ours but, due to their challenging schedules and dedication to their education, they are unwilling to fall in love before graduation. Consider this my prescription to you:

Most women know what attracts them to a particular type of man. It could be the color of his hair or eyes, his height, weight, a particular body measurement, sense of humor, behavior or—most probably—his shoes. So how this works is if you are attracted to tall, dark men, choose for your target an average-sized guy with lighter coloring. If you like muscles, go for a wiry guy instead. If you like Oxfords, pick a guy with loafers (but make him take them off in bed). In other words, no matter what the attraction is, try your best to avoid it to the extent that you're still interested in sleeping with the guy—and nothing more. See? Mom was right…I should have gone to medical school!

If you have enough discipline and will power, you can always target a guy who ticks off all the boxes on your "attractiveness list." (I know you have one! *All* women do.)

However, if you do not possess discipline and will power,

you will be best served by choosing a partner who does not quite meet your usual standards or specifications; he doesn't have to have a hump, but he doesn't need to be Brad Pitt, either. The one-night stand will still be fun, and your husband or boyfriend will still look good to you the next morning!

Role Play

This is my favorite part of *Golden Rule #2* because it sounds so kinky. But the point about role-playing isn't that you should dress up as a naughty nurse or schoolgirl (though, as a man, I do believe that all women should own those costumes and be encouraged to use them often). The idea of playing a role is that your affair shouldn't get too personal.

Golden Rule #1 discussed ways to fake your identity in order to keep your information private. But this *Golden Rule* is stressing how adopting a persona different than your own will help you keep your emotions in check. You know how, when you go on a first date, the best advice you can get is, "Just be yourself"? Well, this isn't about first dates and "getting to know someone." This is about a one-time fling and forgetting you ever knew him!

Part of compartmentalizing is knowing what to keep to yourself. Your home life, your true self and feelings, your partner and what the two of you have together are off-limits. Sex is about exchanging bodily fluids, not personal information. So to keep your real life separate from this short-term diversion it's best to play a role other than yourself.

Men do it all the time. Have you ever noticed how married or otherwise committed men behave differently around women than men who are single? Guys who are married or involved unintentionally give their status away to women almost immediately by how they dress, carry themselves, talk and act all during a short encounter. No wedding ring necessary.

Men who are taken are usually tentative, stick to small talk, and have no "game" at all because they have been away from the dating scene for a long time. They look guilty, act uncomfortable and *smell* married. Single men, on other hand, are generally sharp, have great lines, are aggressive and reek of confidence.

So the smart married man looking for a one-night stand will have done his homework, honed his skills and adopted the personality and mannerisms of a single guy. Well, the same goes for women.

When you spot a potential target, you need to disassociate from your everyday life and adopt the persona of a single woman (even your former, pre-attached self). Be fun, be lighthearted, don't dwell on serious issues (marriage, children, mortgage) and be sure to deflect questions that are too personal or pointed (such as where you live or work but be prepared to use your fake identity if necessary). Keep yourself rooted in this role the whole time you spend together with your new friend. Then when you come back home to your significant other, step back into reality. It keeps the two areas of your life separate and distinct and, in a way, you haven't shared what really matters most—your true self—with anyone but your partner.

How to Keep the Other Man from Falling in Love with You

For most of my lovely, sexy readers, I realize all too well that this section will be one of the most difficult to follow. After all, what man in his right mind would not fall in love with you, especially after a night of passion and complete bliss? That's why it's necessary for you women to cut back on your natural charm when you're having a one-night stand. The question is: how in the hell is that even possible?

Flirting is all part of the fun…but don't be too good at it. If he talks about how much he likes football, don't automatically say how much you love it, too. The man just might propose to you on the spot. Let him know that there's an attraction but not a deep connection. Be the woman he wants to bring to bed, not the one he wants to take home to Mom.

Along the same lines, do not make any sort of plans with him for the future no matter how short-term. If he talks about meeting up next weekend, go with any excuse. If he talks about vacationing together next summer, go out the nearest fire escape.

If you make it impossible for him to contact you—no cell number, no email address, no Facebook account—he'll get the message…and your significant other will not get any kind of incriminating message left on your voicemail. Do not take chances with any form of communication, especially since guys tend to text and booty call anyone on their "contacts" list at 2 a.m., when the bars are closing and you're in bed with your partner.

The attention and flattery that we get from an affair is part of the reason we do it—men and women both. And sometimes it's hard to walk away from someone who strokes your ego and, in addition, other parts of your body that your partner seems to have forgotten about. In fact, the ego boost can be the most downright addictive part of infidelity, especially if you're feeling a lack of affection or appreciation at home. Don't let the attention or sweet words from a stranger steer you off course. Show self-discipline. Stick to the plan. Remind yourself that you want to stay in your relationship. And if the other man seems to be falling for you anyway, well, you can't really blame him—but you've got to cut him loose.

The Strength to Walk Away

The final *Golden Rule* in this book will go into detail about exactly how to man up (sorry, ladies; it's just an expression) and end the affair. But this rule is more concerned with keeping an expiration date in mind, having the will power to stick with it and simply walking away. After all, it's pretty difficult to get serious about—let alone fall in love with—someone whom you know is only a temporary distraction in your life. Your relationship with your significant other is the final destination; your one-night stand should merely be a short but pleasant layover.

Of course, walking away from a seemingly good thing—good sex, a good time, a good night…or all three at once—is never easy. It requires the serious self-discipline that we discussed and practiced earlier in this chapter. You've got to always keep the expiration date in mind and stick to it; after that, a fling is just like spoiled milk. One whiff will tell you not to take another taste. That's why, if you are determined to cheat on your significant other, you must develop your will power; otherwise, you will not have enough strength to carry out your plan and call an end to the affair.

The best practice for improving will power is to carry out certain tasks or activities that you would rather avoid doing due to lack of desire, laziness, procrastination, weakness, shyness, etc. Think of boot camp training, waking up for work or visiting your in-laws every weekend. When you repeatedly perform tasks that you don't want to do, you overcome your subconscious resistance to doing them, and they become more like second nature to you after a while.

The following exercises will help improve your will power, giving you the strength to walk away from an affair even when you don't want to.

GOLDEN RULE#2: KEEP THE "LOVE" OUT OF "LOVE AFFAIR"

☞ If you drink three cups of coffee every day, cut that down to only one cup. Or if you usually take milk or sugar, drink your coffee black.

☞ If you wake up at 7:00 a.m. each morning, set your alarm to get up at 6:15 a.m. even on weekends.

☞ If you exercise for one hour several times a week, increase that to an hour and a half.

☞ If you have a nightly habit of watching TV to relax, force yourself to skip it.

In a short amount of time, you will learn to do unpleasant tasks—though no one says you have to like it! That will also give you the confidence in your own will power to end the affair or not allow a one-night stand to last more than one night. (Note: there's a reason it's not called a "one-month stand" or an "I'll-just-stay-for-breakfast stand." Will power, people!) Also notice that you'll have kicked the sugar and caffeine habit, gotten in better shape, become more productive in the mornings and reduced your TV viewing. These are all beneficial goals, much like saving your current relationship and not giving in to short-term—and possibly destructive—desires.

Though *Golden Rule #2* involves discipline, strength and will power, it comes down to something really quite simple: if you're looking for a good time, leave love out of it.

Case Study #2

Since the importance of *Golden Rule #2* cannot be overstated, let's review it by studying and comparing two real-life scenarios involving Jennifer and Samantha.

A few years back, when Jennifer was still married, she met a young intern while visiting her sick cousin at a Seattle hospital. The two of them quickly hit it off since Jen was spending a lot of time at the hospital. They seemed to have a lot in common despite their age difference; Jen was eight years older.

One day, before his shift ended, the intern came to Jen's cousin's room to check up on his patient one more time. After a while, Jen and the intern left the hospital together, and he asked Jen if she wanted to get something to eat before she went home. She agreed, and the two went for dinner in a nearby restaurant.

They ended up in his apartment, and the two spent the night making passionate love. Jen was delighted with the opportunity to meet such a wonderful young man, especially one who seemed so interested in her when she was feeling particularly low.

As usual, Jen's fling was unplanned, and decisions were made without much thought for the consequences. To that end she spent the next several evenings with the guy, going out to dinner, movies and even a couple of nightclubs. Jen was trying to prove to herself and the young intern that she could keep up with him regardless of the age difference.

To spend so much time with someone other than your own husband or boyfriend creates so many different issues, such as attachment and the development of feelings by either party. After a short while, these can become difficult to manage and conceal.

For her part, Jen was starting to have some emotional attachment to her new friend. For one thing, she was alone in a strange city and was feeling a bit vulnerable due to her cousin's condition. But she knew in the back of her mind that she'd be leaving soon.

Of course, Jen didn't confess that she was a married woman, which led the young intern to think that she could be interested in a long-term relationship. As a result, he developed strong feelings for her in a short span of time.

When the week was over, Jen packed for home— but, allowing her feelings to get the best of her, she took the guy's phone number and vowed to stay in touch with him when she got back.

But to Jen's surprise, it took him only thirty-six hours to call her at her place of work. She freaked out a little when she heard his voice, wondering how he had gotten her number. It was easy. She had given him her real name and had told him where she lived. The rest of the information was already out there, just waiting to be Googled.

However, the intern was obviously offended by her reaction, expecting a warmer reception. He anticipated that she would be pleasantly surprised by his initiative to contact her, and he became upset and angry at her aloofness, which caught Jen off-guard. It was only then that she realized what a mistake she had made by spending so much time with this young guy, allowing him to become emotionally involved and attached.

This no longer was a case of boosting her spirit and her ego; it was downright scary. How would she get rid of him now? Jen blamed herself for being so careless and undisciplined, but she did not know what to do and had no one to turn to for advice.

The following day, the intern called again, but this time Jen didn't answer. She realized that his aggressiveness might not fade any time soon and recognized that she was in big trouble and somehow had to distance herself from him as quickly as possible.

When he called the third time, Jen seized the moment and, figuring a way to get him to stop calling, informed him that she was coming back to Seattle to see him the next weekend. He got excited, knowing what was in store for him, and was eager to see her again so soon.

When they met in Seattle, the young intern's emotions took over; without any hesitation he told Jen that he was falling in love with her. Jen was astonished and didn't know how to react to his admission. She knew deep inside that there was no future between them and figured it was best to tell him that and terminate the relationship as quickly as possible before the affair became unmanageable.

Jen gently tried to defuse the situation by taking the blame for leading him on. She used the age and geographical differences between them as "deal breakers," but the guy was not convinced and would not take no for an answer.

Jen was scared; she was running out of options. She never had planned for such an event and was consequently not prepared to handle the circumstances as swiftly and deftly as she should have. She finally decided to tell the truth and to end the relationship immediately, informing the young man that she was married and could no longer see or be in contact with him. She offered an apology and left Seattle the next day, hoping to return to her normal life with her husband.

A few days later, the intern called Jen's workplace once again and informed her that after careful consideration and evaluation of his feelings toward her, he'd be comfortable sharing her with her husband. The two of them could meet in Seattle, or he offered to fly out to be with her on occasion, but complete separation from her was not an option he'd consider.

Jen was very panicked now. The guy would not leave her alone, and it began to feel like he was a stalker. She told him that while his plan might be an attractive arrangement for them in the short term, eventually he would want more from the relationship, and she could not afford to comply since she was already married. The guy did not want to hear any of it.

With no alternative, Jen decided to let things work themselves out. She did not want to face the mess she had created due to her own lack of planning and self-discipline in her involvement with the intern. Instead, she chose to ignore his calls and hope he'd get the point.

Several weeks passed, and on a Friday afternoon, as Jen left her office, she saw the intern outside in a rental car, waiting for her. She became extremely angry and decided that the time had come to make a harsh and abrupt break from this guy since things were getting out of hand. Secure in the fact that it was still daylight and that other people were around, she walked straight up and informed him that she had hired an attorney and would obtain a restraining order against him. Furthermore, she said she had requested the attorney to submit a copy to his employer at the hospital and submit a formal complaint against him in an attempt to discourage him from following and harassing her.

Jen's threat worked; due to the fear of losing his position, he promised to stay away and part ways with Jen once and for all. In return, Jen promised not to file the restraining order so that his record would remain unblemished. It was far from a clean break, but it was the best solution she could come up with after having made so many mistakes.

If we explore the reason Jen did not break off her relationship with the intern right after their first night of intimacy, it becomes clear that she enjoyed his company as well as the sex. She did not keep her feelings under control, and instead allowed her emotions to play too big a role. The "proper" procedure, according to *Golden Rule #2*, would have been to have the one-night stand and then stop seeing the intern at the hospital (his schedule was posted) and avoid all contact with him for the remainder of her stay. Soon, he would have discovered Jen's true motive all along, which was casual sex with no further involvement.

Jen learned the valuable lesson that emotions have no place in an affair. But that lesson could have cost her a whole lot more in attorneys' fees and the possibility of losing her husband.

Now let's take a look at Samantha, who applied the practical approach of The 9 Golden Rules (in particular *Golden Rule #2*) when she volunteered to go to a work conference in Dallas. After checking into her hotel, she befriended one of the female staff members there and lightheartedly asked for a good nightlife spot in the area.

After arriving at the restaurant/lounge and having a drink, she noticed a good-looking guy with a great physique. She smiled at him, and he approached her almost immediately. The two got acquainted remarkably well in a short period of time, and they spent the rest of the evening together at his place making passionate love.

After the encounter, she was tempted to spend the night, but she knew she couldn't give in to her short-term feelings. Instead, she said goodbye—giving no further indication that they'd meet again. She arrived at her hotel room around 3:30 a.m. and noticed that the red light on the phone was flashing, indicating that she had a message. It was her husband checking up on her. Sam knew not to panic since she had an alibi already in place. She called the front desk, requested an 8:00 a.m. wake-up call and went to bed.

The next morning, Sam called her husband at 8:15 local time, which was two hours ahead of Malibu, where they resided. Her husband, of course, was still half-asleep when he picked up the phone and asked, "Where were you last night?" Sam responded that she had gone to bed early and had disconnected the phone to get a decent night's sleep because she had a lot of work ahead of her today. She had done that before on other business trips as well.

Let's consider the way Sam kept her cool—and kept her marriage together—by keeping her emotions under control and sticking with her original plan.

First, she volunteered to go to Dallas with the intention of having a one-night stand. That gave her plenty of time to figure out details and alibis beforehand, and she knew she wouldn't be caught off-guard by the first tall, dark and handsome stranger she met. She'd be ready for him!

Next, even though Sam and her target really hit it off, she didn't reveal any personal information that he could use to trace her once she was back home. Along those lines, she refused to take his business card or give him hers, explaining that long-distance relationships "never worked" for her. When he asked if he could see her again during her stay, she told him that she was leaving Dallas early the next day (which explained why she had to get back to the hotel). Also, as much as she would have liked to, she didn't allow any impulsive actions to keep her at his place longer than the time allotted in her plan.

Third, she had an alibi already awaiting her husband, and she didn't let her nerves or emotions get the better of her when he confronted her (by calling when he was still asleep, she also gave herself the upper hand in case of a potential argument). In fact, she had prepared a pattern of leaving her phone turned off during other business trips (whether she was having an affair or not) to set a precedent for an occasion such as this one to make the story more believable. Her husband was satisfied with her explanation—and she was more than satisfied with her one-night stand!

#3

Never with Someone You Know

The majority of married or involved people who commit adultery do so with someone they know, such as a coworker, a neighbor or a friend's fiancé. In case you haven't noticed, the majority are also the ones getting caught!

Sure, cheating with someone you already know can be convenient, quick and easy, especially for those who are not freely available to meet strangers at bars or other social places. But convenience isn't always all it's cracked up to be. We're not talking about picking up your dinner at a drive-thru window. We're talking about picking up someone to have an affair with! And that takes planning and precaution.

One of the problems with having a fling with someone you know is that it is often an unplanned, spur-of-the-moment type of thing. After all, it is difficult to resist repeated temptation—especially when it is constantly in your face...or in the office just down the hall. Usually under these circumstances, the irrevocable act of infidelity takes place without warning or planning—and mistakes are made. You must avoid those temptations and remove yourself from situations where such a possibility can present itself. It all goes back to *Golden Rule #1*: If you don't want to get caught, you've got to plan ahead.

It is not difficult to see how those cheating with someone they know are likely to get caught. What is difficult to believe is that they feel surprised and shocked when they inevitably *do* get caught! The chances of getting trapped in such an affair and the whole disaster being discovered by your loved one increase exponentially when a known party is involved—and with such a high probability, why any woman would put herself in harm's way is beyond comprehension. (And, no, "having emotions" is no excuse; see *Golden Rule #2* again.)

Since the two of you are already acquainted with each other, your new companion knows everything about you, such as where you live, where you work, your phone numbers and so forth. How scary is that? Your so-called "one-night stand" knows you and your schedule so well that he can practically predict your every move. Therefore, there is no escape route, no possibility of a false identity or denial and, most dangerous of all, you are at his mercy when it comes to keeping your secret from your loved one.

If you use such bad judgment and trap yourself by sleeping with someone you know, all you can do is hope that he does not have real feelings for you or that the quality of your sexual encounter was so poor that he doesn't want to continue the relationship. Some choice, huh?

So in the interest of keeping your real relationship alive, I want you to think of this chapter as a "guy guide": those you can consider as targets and those who are absolutely out of the question. Remember—when it comes to affairs, a perfect stranger can sometimes be a girl's best friend.

Getting Friendly with His Friends

Okay, so you find most of his beer buddies, sports buddies and work buddies immature or just plain repulsive. And who can blame you? Most of us guys are guilty as charged. But there may be that *one*—his friend who laughs at your jokes, listens to what you say and has somehow evolved enough to know how to treat a lady—who you wouldn't mind getting a bit friendly with yourself. You already know him, he seems to like you and you know he'll keep his mouth shut because he values your man's friendship. A perfect target, right?

Sure, except for one thing. Well, three things:

☞ You already know him, which makes him hard to get rid of afterward.

☞ He *does* like you, which makes him hard to get rid of afterward.

☞ And he doesn't value your man's friendship half as much as he'd value continuing to be your friend with unlimited benefits.

So let me make this perfectly clear: sleeping with one of his friends is *never* a good idea.

By having a fling with one of his buddies, you'd be breaking a majority of **The 9 Golden Rules** that we've already covered: it's too close to home, he knows your identity (not to mention your address, your personal information and—oh, yeah!—your man) and there are emotions involved. Walking away from the affair would be almost impossible considering he's probably on your couch every Sunday with your significant other, watching the game. And what do you think would happen if there were ever a falling out between the two of them? Do the words, "I slept with your wife/girlfriend?" give you any kind of clue?

Also, I'm not sure if you know this, ladies, but guys talk; we can't keep any secrets, and we are worse than women when it comes to gossip, especially when it involves sex. Your target may not necessarily tell your significant other about your fling, but it's practically guaranteed that he'll blab (i.e., brag) to some of their other buddies about it. Then it's only a matter of time—and perhaps a few six-packs—before the news makes its way to your man's ears. End of friendship. End of relationship. End of story.

All in the Family

Have you ever been to a family function with your significant other and noticed how much his younger brother resembles him—only with more in the hair department and less in the way of love handles? Maybe the thought entered your mind that having a fling with the brother wouldn't really be cheating since it's more like revisiting the former version of your husband/boyfriend when the two of you first met. To that I say, "Nice try, but I'm not buying it."

Having an affair with a member of your boyfriend or husband's family (and, yes, that includes in-laws, step-brothers/fathers, adopted or estranged siblings and even second cousins) is quite possibly the worst choice you could make. Not only is it somewhat incestuous, it's just plain icky—and it goes against all of the proven strategies set forth in The 9 Golden Rules.

They say that blood is thicker than water, and while I'm not quite sure what that comparison is supposed to mean, one thing is certain: eventually, when the loyalty among relatives—if not sibling rivalry or the desire for revenge—wins out, the family member you chose as your target will spill his guts—or gloat or write it in a Christmas card for all to see—that he slept with you. You will lose your man for sure and maybe even break up his family. On the bright side, you won't ever have to see his mother again.

Even if the truth doesn't come out at first, there will always be the threat at every family function that the relative you slept with will let your secret slip. If you dreaded get-togethers with your man's family before, just imagine how much worse it will be from that point on. That thought alone should be enough to convince you that, while his brother may be easy access, he is definitely off-limits.

Business or Coach?

We're not talking about flights here but flings. Business and coach are both out of the question, "business" being anyone with whom you or your man works (colleagues, bosses, business associates, customers) and "coach" referring to anyone who comes in contact with your kids (coaches, teachers, the parents of your children's friends, fellow PTA members, etc.), if you have any.

First of all, affairs in the workplace wreak havoc on two fronts: personal and professional. As we've noted, the temptation to target someone in the same office is great—sometimes overwhelming. And that's a sure sign to walk away since it shows that your judgment is already getting cloudy.

One red flag is that you spend too much of your time with coworkers as it is, sometimes more than you spend with your spouse or significant other. You already have an established relationship together, and that can lead to all kinds of emotions, especially after you've slept together.

Office affairs are particularly hard to walk away from. Unless you're prepared to quit your job, you'll most likely see your one-night stand from Friday first thing bright and early on Monday morning…and every weekday after that. He'll call your work extension, he'll email, he may even schedule his coffee breaks to coincide with yours. Try as you might, you cannot avoid interacting with him.

Before you know it, the balance may shift, and your "office relationship" could start seeming more real than the one you have at home. Soon you may dread the weekends and find yourself volunteering for overtime—and it won't go unnoticed by your man. You may be able to slip a few fake orgasms past him, but no one is that good of an actress that she can hide her feelings on a consistent basis. And it won't be long before your significant other hands you your walking papers.

Second, unless you're involved in the world's oldest profession, sex and business don't mix. Carrying on an affair in the workplace can ruin your focus, concentration and self-discipline on the job as well as at home, which is how most people slip up and get caught cheating. It can also start a flurry of office gossip and speculation, which could not only ruin your reputation professionally but also get back to your man.

If you target one of your husband or boyfriend's colleagues or business associates, things can get even uglier. He'll hear the gossip firsthand, and you'll hurt him in the worst possible way, making him appear weak, powerless and clueless in front of his peers. Remember, the point of the fling is to have fun and enjoy yourself, not to hurt those you love.

For the same reason, if you have kids, their coaches/teachers/best friends' dads are not even an option—and that goes for the best friend, too, even if he is of legal age.

After your third parent-teacher conference in a week or the fact that the soccer coach chose you as his new assistant because you're an excellent ball handler, rumors will spread around the community like wildfire, and your children will eventually hear that their mother's a "slut" (don't cringe—kids can be cruel).

If you decide to pull a Mrs. Robinson and school your teenage son's best friend on the finer points of life, don't expect such a young cub to be able to keep his mouth closed. Just as quickly as he came, he'll be shooting out texts to all of his friends in no time, and your teenager will hear about it. Just hope there's no footage floating around on YouTube.

To keep your family together, keep your knees together when it comes to coaches, teachers, classmates' parents or your teenagers' friends.

Never the Same Man Twice

The advantage of creating a false identity and committing adultery with someone you don't know is similar to how a spy character in a movie always calculates her next move, works from a plan, has an escape route figured out in advance and never gets caught. Spies won't even enter a room without first knowing that there are at least two exits.

But by having a one-night stand more than once with the same person, you're blocking your own escape route and throwing away the key. In other words, you're taking unnecessary chances.

No matter how tempting and appealing it is, avoid having sexual encounters repeatedly with the same man. There are, after all, many issues and concerns that can emerge from continued intimacy with a partner. Recycling a fling may be easy, but eventually the emotions will come—and as we learned in the last chapter, emotions are the enemy.

Emotions have been developed over the years to function as an internal guidance system that impacts our decision-making ability and its direction. Many experts believe that emotions influence our brain in making decisions and that the two are interconnected. This is very possible since we, as humans, often can't make choices unless we have some feelings connected to them one way or another.

For instance, suppose you plan to purchase a car and, after reviewing all the details and comparisons, it comes down to choosing between two different makes and models. From a technical and financial standpoint, the two are extremely comparable to each other, so which one do you choose? Most probably you will choose the one that makes you feel good when you look at it or picture yourself in it. Hence, at the end of all logical analyses that you performed, the final decision rests on your emotions. (And, no, I'm not just talking about women here. Men have been known to fall in love with their "baby"…excuse me, I mean "car.")

When it comes to infidelity, your emotions must be disconnected from your decisions and be more in line with your pre-planned goals and agenda (i.e., cheating successfully and keeping your relationship intact). You must practice self-control and awareness because these are the qualities that will assist you in acting rather than *re*acting, and eliminating sudden impulses from your brain so that you are more in control of your actions and external events.

Of course, the best way to keep emotions out of it is to avoid sleeping with the same target twice. Doing so can cause a multitude of problems, including:

☞ Even if you didn't know him initially and created an alias, you will eventually expose your true identity.

☞ You can develop an addiction to intimacy with the other man.

☞ You may acquire a new taste.

☞ You may develop strong emotions for someone other than your boyfriend/spouse.

☞ You may find yourself constantly making plans to see the other man.

☞ There will be a preoccupation with the "what ifs."

Let's examine each of these issues in depth to understand why multiple sexual encounters with the same man are hazardous to your marriage or relationship.

☞ Even if you didn't know him initially and created an alias, you will eventually expose your true identity.

The false identity you developed works well when it is used properly, which is optimally when you are out of town and you plan to never see your one-night stand again. But if you break these rules, it is quite possible that your lies and deception—as well as your true identity—will be exposed since it is difficult to live a double life for an extended period of time. Once your target knows the true you, he can contact you easily in attempts to continue the affair, putting your relationship with your loved one at risk.

☞ You can develop an addiction to intimacy
with the other man.

The addiction to sex with someone new in your life is like any other addiction: a strong, persistent behavioral pattern marked by physical and/or psychological dependency that causes significant disruption and negatively impacts your quality of life. Doesn't sound too sexy, does it? This compulsive behavior will cloud your judgment and cause damage to your already existing relationship.

The lack of control you experience over your own wants and emotions will cause you to commit errors in your decision-making process, which will trigger undisciplined behavior that leads to carelessness and mistakes. Eventually your significant other will discover your infidelity—but by then your addiction may be wearing off, and you'll realize that it was so not worth it.

☞ You may acquire a new taste.

This is an interesting but dangerous phenomenon. Let's assume you had sex with a young man, perhaps five to ten years younger than your husband or boyfriend. He had a strong, muscular physique and was sexually far more pleasing than your significant other.

Even if you did not fall in love with him, you tasted a different flavor that you liked better than the usual one. Since you had a new sexual experience, it could be difficult if not impossible for you to enjoy sex with your spouse or companion the same way again.

You may start to avoid intimacy with your usual partner because you are not as aroused anymore, or you may try to teach your old dog new tricks (suddenly switching to reverse cowgirl from the usual missionary style you've been enjoying all these years is a sure sign). All of this will lead to suspicion on your man's part—and, most often, this is the beginning of the end. He will become more jealous and suspicious of your activities, especially the time you spend away from home. As a result, the bell will ring, the gloves will come on and constant fighting will begin until it becomes unbearable. You will either confess your indiscretions or give up on the relationship altogether—often with the same result.

☞ You may develop strong emotions for someone other than your boyfriend/spouse.

If you have multiple sexual encounters with another man, there is a strong possibility that you will develop feelings for him. The emotions you will experience could be lust, infatuation, sexual addiction or love—it's hard to tell the difference at times, and you may not even want to at any one time.

But how can you develop feelings for someone other than your husband or boyfriend at the same time? Is that even possible? Yes. Is this a risk you can afford to take? No.

Developing any kind of feelings for the other man is not a chance that a married or involved woman should take, and the most practical approach is to stop seeing him after the first sexual encounter.

☞ You may find yourself constantly making plans to see the other man.

As your feelings for the other man get stronger, your desire to see him more often will take over your mental and emotional state. Such desperation could affect your ability to function and make proper decisions, adversely affecting your marriage or relationship.

Once love or lust has taken over the majority of your brain's power to function, the detailed planning, self-discipline and will power required to succeed in cheating on your boyfriend/ spouse are no longer valid tools that you can employ. *Strategic calm* has, alas, given way to *schoolgirl crush*.

Your constant desire to see your new partner will eventually expose you. As your alibis become less believable and you slip up more and more in your eagerness, your significant other will detect abnormality in your daily routine and emotional state. This will ultimately lead to confrontation, which could be followed by divorce or separation.

☞ There will be a preoccupation with the "what ifs."

When you get involved with another person, despite all the cautions and warnings, most women (and men, for that matter) will tend to daydream and become preoccupied with the "what ifs." *What if we end up together? What if he's the one I'm supposed to be with?*

This simple act of daydreaming can cause you to remove yourself from the reality of your everyday life to the extent that you may start to see your spouse or significant other as an obstacle to your true happiness. In your mind, your life partner suddenly becomes the "other man," and your fling takes center stage. You may even start to resent your significant other for keeping you away from your new "love," and separation is sure to follow. The only problem is that you may have made a huge mistake.

Some women try to convince themselves that "having an affair" is somehow different than having a one-night stand. They feel that seeing the same man a couple of times is sweeter and less "slutty" than sleeping with him once. But romance is the point of *fidelity*, not *in*fidelity.

Falling Out of Love with Your Loved One

Some married or committed women enjoy the novelty of sex when it involves intimacy with a stranger as long as he is different than what she is used to and there is sufficient sexual attraction between them. These women are the lucky ones; they usually do not develop feelings for or an attachment to their sexual partner.

On the other hand, there are some married or involved women who allow their emotions to affect them after their affair, and they lose sight of their original objective. To lose focus and control by developing feelings for the other man should be considered against the official rules of engagement and must be avoided at all costs. Consider it a threat to your life and your lifestyle since these emotions cannot easily be veiled or hidden from your partner. They usually grow with time (and with each time you sleep with the same man) and will affect your ability to make appropriate decisions and carry out your original intentions.

You will surely get caught cheating since your emotions will control your actions and thoughts; each time you see the other man, your grip on managing the affair will get weaker and weaker until you are exposed. Or, if you are the type of woman who finds it difficult to control your feelings, you may soon fall out of love with your boyfriend or husband, and the relationship that you worked so hard to build together will end abruptly and often, once the emotions settle, for no good reason.

Therefore, the best and simplest practice to avoid dealing with these emotions and the fear of falling out of love with your significant other is to avoid repeated intimacy with the same man. You must avoid further contact with him and all thoughts that concern him. Regardless of how attractive and appealing he is to you, if you know you will never see him again, the chances of developing feelings for him or falling in love with him are quite remote.

To increase your chances of never seeing the other man again and keeping your marriage or relationship intact, here is a list of guys you *must* avoid having any sexual thoughts or feelings about or any physical contact with:

☞ Any of your man's friends

☞ Any of his relatives

☞ His coworkers/boss/business associates

☞ Your coworkers/boss/business associates

☞ Any neighbor

☞ Any fellow PTA member

☞ Your kid's teacher/coach

☞ Your friend's husband or boyfriend

Remember that when you commit adultery with someone you know, you are at the mercy of many elements (including your emotions) that are out of your control—not to mention the individual with whom you had casual sex.

But if you are still considering committing infidelity with someone you know, here are a few questions you should have answers for prior to the act:

☞ Do you know his motives?

☞ Do you know what he wants/expects out of the relationship?

☞ Will it be awkward seeing him again, especially on a regular basis and with your significant other there as well?

☞ Will he hold the affair over your head as a form of emotional blackmail?

☞ Can you consider or afford having a relationship with him?

If you're not sure about the answers or think that the outcome may be negative, find a new target farther from your home and further from your heart. After all, you went into this thing with two objectives: to have a little fun, and to keep your current relationship intact. Becoming divorced or separated accomplishes neither of those. Neither does ending a friendship, estranging your man from his relative, humiliating yourself or your family or causing problems in the workplace.

Even with all of your planning and will power, there is a certain amount of unpredictability in any affair or one-night stand. But in the case of choosing a target, the devil you *don't* know is definitely better than the devil you do.

Case Study #3

To appreciate the importance of *Golden Rule #3*, let's take a look at Samantha, who broke the rule but then applied it in time when she was on a golf vacation in Florida with a few associates. There she noticed Joe, whom she had met six months earlier on a business trip to Ohio. Sam was pleasantly surprised to see him, but there was a slight problem: during their last encounter, there had been a lot of flirting followed by a one-night stand—though she had managed to keep her full identity and marital status under wraps at the time.

She knew it was a dangerous thing to do, but she broke the "never-the-same-man-twice" rule when he asked her out again. The opportunity seemed too good to pass up, and, for once, she let her emotions take over.

Sam spent the next several days with Joe and avoided all contact with friends and any of the people she knew in Florida who could reveal her true identity. This time somehow felt different; she had cheated on her husband before but had never inadvertently run into someone with whom she enjoyed spending time as much as Joe. The great sexual experiences they had were too powerful to ignore, and she wanted more.

It didn't take long for Sam's self-discipline to disappear. She quickly lost sight of her reason for being in Florida in the first place: to play golf with friends—some of whom knew her husband. Unlike other trips on which she planned to commit adultery, this one was merely supposed to be a fun and relaxing sporting event; infidelity was never part of the original agenda.

Although Sam felt herself developing feelings for Joe, to her absolute credit she recognized how out of character her behavior was, and she realized that she had to resist the emotions she was experiencing. Two days before her departure, she knew that she had to break off the relationship before it got out of hand, so she called and asked him for a lunch date.

During their meeting, she made up a story that she had been seeing someone for the past six months (just after she had first met Joe), and they were currently on a break to sort things out. Sam said that the man had previously gotten out of a long-term relationship and wasn't sure he was ready for another one. However, she said that he called her last night and decided that he'd like to get back together and give their relationship a go.

"So I agreed," explained Sam. "I'm going to see him back home on Sunday."

During this speech, Sam held Joe's hand, looked into his eyes as passionately as she could, and she continued. "These past several days that I spent with you were magnificent. You made me feel like a woman again. I'm lucky to have run into you. This was surely destiny."

Though the reality was far different, Sam meant most of what she said—and Joe left there with the feeling that she was a genuine lady of good character. Sam was able to save face and her marriage at the same time. But she learned a truly valuable lesson that even the most experienced adulterer can get burned by re-igniting an old flame.

Compare the example above to Jennifer, who was still married to her first husband when she went out one night to a bachelorette party. There were altogether ten women in the group, and they started going club-hopping to different bars. By 11:30, things got rowdy when they ended up at a male revue strip club.

The evening soon stretched into the early hours of the morning, and while the celebration was in full swing, Jen noticed one of the entertainers in particular. A bit buzzed, she gave him a good tip and then requested some private time to get to know him better. She bought the young man a few drinks, and the attraction between them became apparent.

It turned out that the dancer was a twenty-four year old college student. He claimed to be working in such an environment because he couldn't afford his tuition and all he was trying to do was earn enough money to work his way through his final year of college. Jen was moved by his story—not to mention infatuated with his physique. They parted ways soon after, but Jen couldn't get him out of her mind.

The next week, knowing her new friend's schedule, Jen left work and went back to the male revue to see him. She sat in the first row to ensure that he noticed her; they made eye contact and, shortly thereafter, followed the same routine as the previous time.

The interest that this young man was showing in Jen started to generate a set of emotions that soon obscured her reality: namely, that she was a married woman. They soon started seeing each other regularly at the club on all the nights he performed.

After a little over two weeks of seeing each other, Jen told her husband that she had a one-day business trip and managed to spend the night together with her new flame. She came home the next day triumphant, claiming that there might be a few more possible day trips in the near future.

The problem was that Jen could not get this guy out of her mind—nor did she want to. She developed feelings for him and couldn't wait to be back with him as soon as she could: the sex was amazing, the conversation was playful and they always seemed to have a great time. Jen felt like she was in college again.

These emotions prevented her from thinking coherently and with an objective. No matter how exciting things were at the moment, she had to realize that she shouldn't have been seeing him repeatedly and that their "relationship" could not possibly last a long time.

Jen had committed a cardinal sin. As a married woman, if she wished to cheat on her husband, she should have acted quickly and decisively, not drag out a one-night-stand to the point where she felt she was falling in love with another man. However, she couldn't convince herself that the "infatuation" she was feeling was based merely on physical attraction and not love—and getting together with the object of her desire again and again made it only worse.

She continued to see the dancer for another six months until he finished college and moved back East. Luckily, her husband never found out about the affair. But he divorced her nonetheless because it became obvious that she had let herself lose all interest in him.

After stuffing so many dollar bills in the young man's briefs, Jen was left with less money in her bank account and no one waiting for her at home.

GOLDEN RULE

#4

Hide the Evidence

Let's face it: "lie" is such an ugly word. So let's use "hide the evidence" instead. The term has been used by politicians and presidents of companies when they screw people over, so it should work just fine for screwing someone other than your man.

Whatever we choose to call it, *Golden Rule #4* is a necessary step in having an affair. It will help you hide any evidence—

from where you've been all those hours (hopefully that's plural; otherwise you've picked the wrong guy for a satisfying one-night stand) to ditching the bling given to you by your new fling. (Yes, you may have earned it, but no, you cannot keep it.)

To cheat successfully, every little thing counts and is crucial. Imagine what overlooking even one small piece of evidence can do to your relationship. Cover your tracks and keep in mind that when it comes to affairs, there's no room for amateur mistakes.

Accounting for Your Absences

If you're married or in a long-term relationship, you've definitely developed a certain set of habits regarding your daily schedule and time together. For many, this routine is a source of comfort and stability. For others, it's a rut and part of the reason they want to have an affair in the first place. Either way, such long-established patterns are hard to break, and any change may be met with discomfort or downright suspicion from your significant other.

Basically, any woman looking to step out temporarily has two choices: she either maintains her routine with her partner while creating some free time elsewhere, or she breaks her routine—even if it's just for one passionate rendezvous—and accounts for her absences without arousing her man's distrust. How? The answer is simple: always plan ahead.

Maintaining Your Routine

Have you ever looked at your full-time job as offering you freedom and flexibility? Well, it does when it comes to "afternoon delights."

One of the best ways to maintain your normal schedule

with your man is to take a little time off work. Make sure it's nothing drastic that will catch your coworkers' attention; after all, you don't want them calling your home or running into your significant other and asking if you're all right because you've been taking a lot of sick days lately—plus, if you're having an affair, you probably *have* been looking a little flush with excitement…and it's not the flu that's causing it. Taking an extra hour for, ahem, "lunch" or, on occasion, working through breaks at your desk and then popping out of the office an hour or two early will give you enough time for a well-planned tryst. You can have your fun and still be home for dinner at the usual time without skipping a beat. Who says you can't have your cake and eat it too?

Of course, if your significant other is in the habit of dropping by your office for an unexpected visit or surprise lunchtime invitation, those options may be out the window. But since there aren't too many men who do that—let alone ever even consider doing that—it won't be a problem. And we men wonder why women have affairs!

If you don't work and your husband or partner does, that leaves you plenty of time in the day for an adulterous romp. But be sure your timing is right. If he usually calls you from the office, make sure you're not too preoccupied to answer the phone. And if he wonders what you did all day, mention something about shopping or manicures. If he's a typical man, his eyes will glaze over, and he'll pretty much stop listening at that point, much less ask any further questions. But you should also make sure your nails look good just in case he isn't comatose and decides to check.

Breaking Your Routine

This is where planning is essential. In order to keep your schedule as close to normal as possible, you'll need to lay a solid foundation well in advance before even considering a fling. That means no midnight workouts at the gym, no sudden spa weekends, no "emergencies" that kept you late at work (unless, of course, you happen to work in an emergency room; then find your Dr. McDreamy and the nearest supply closet and "play doctor" to your heart's content). But for most of you, you'll need to modify your schedule way ahead of actually carrying out an affair. So I guess now is as good a time as any to sign up for those early morning Pilates classes you've been putting off!

The change in your routine will have to start early and gradually. Establish a new pattern and stick to it for a few months until any suspicion on your partner's part has worn off. For example, if you decide to take a spin class on Wednesday evenings after work, sign up weeks before you consider having an affair. Have your partner check out the gym with you and even pick you up there once or twice. Go to the class directly from your office, return home sweaty in your workout gear, and take a shower immediately. By the time you're ready for your fling, your significant other will be used to the change in your routine—and your legs will look fabulous!

Once you've picked out your target and made a date for your rendezvous, make it a Wednesday night. Skip spin class and go directly to the bar, restaurant or motel where you're supposed to meet. Make sure you have your gym clothes in the car to change into afterward. When you get home sweaty and a bit worse for wear from your one-night stand, your man will think you had a good workout—and hopefully he'll be right! Take a shower, like usual, and all the evidence of your affair will be washed down the drain.

Of course, such a change in your schedule will require strong will power and discipline—both of which will empower you to be in control of your mind, your thoughts, your time and your actions, and thus in control of your affair. This is about risk mitigation and reduction, leaving little to chance. After all, poor decisions and errors usually occur when:

☞ you do things that are out of your norm

☞ you are out of your element

☞ you are out of your environment

☞ you lack sufficient preparation

☞ you do not plan an affair

Remember: additions, subtractions or alterations to any part of your schedule will raise a red flag and put you on your man's radar. The chances of getting caught after making any changes are much greater than at other times, so allow enough time to elapse before altering your patterns and actually committing infidelity. Don't rely on these excuses:

☞ sudden changes to your work schedule

☞ after-work drinks

☞ girls' night out

☞ sporting or social events with friends

☞ out-of-town meetings or gatherings

☞ meeting new friends

Most of the above are one-time-only deals. More than that and they become a bit suspicious.

In the world of adultery, reducing risk and avoiding getting caught are the most significant elements to the survival of your relationship and way of life—and that means putting in the effort and planning ahead. It may seem like a lot of work but, if done right, it'll definitely be worth it.

Learn to Lie

You don't have to like it, but you do have to lie. There's no way to carry out an affair and hide the evidence without it. Imagine the conversations otherwise:

Him: "How was your day, dear?"

You: "Fine. I did the presentation at work, did three miles on the treadmill, did the grocery shopping, did some guy at a motel, did the laundry. And how was your day, darling?"

At best, you're going to have to learn the lie of omission. In other words, have the same conversation as above, only leave out the part about the guy at the motel. Obviously. Oh, and as long as you're at it, might as well make it five miles on the treadmill.

Luckily, learning to lie is not all that difficult. In fact, many women are already good at it. So good in fact that it's scary. Case in point: "You're the best I've ever had, baby," "You're the biggest I've ever had, baby," "That's okay, baby, I didn't feel like having an orgasm tonight anyway." Sound familiar?

The thing about lying convincingly is that it takes practice—and this is where discipline and planning ahead come into play again. Lying is a lot like sex: the best way to become good at it is to start out small and continue doing it until you're comfortable. So my recommendation is that you start out with little white lies well in advance of having an affair. That way, when the time comes to cover your tracks, your mannerisms, pattern of speech and pangs of guilt won't give you away.

As an example, make up a small story about an old female friend you ran into at the grocery store (of course, it should be untraceable). Add details, try for a casual, not too rapid tone, avoid fidgeting and maintain eye contact with your partner the whole time. Afterward, write down some of the information you told him. Put the note away then try to recall all the points you mentioned a few days later. While it's unlikely that your significant other will ask any follow-up questions about this particular incident, it gives you a chance to test your recall. A few days later, lie about an event at work and do the same thing; this should strengthen your memory and improve your ability to maintain your nonchalance.

As you build up your lying technique, start to skip a few sessions at, say, your Wednesday night spin class or whatever time you're planning to have your fling. Do something else instead: go to a movie out of town, have dinner with a girlfriend whom your husband doesn't know. When it's time to go home, change into the gym clothes you kept in your car for exactly this purpose (use a public restroom in a Dunkin' Donuts or even a gas station if need be) and then follow your usual routine. When your man asks how your workout was, answer the way you normally would, neither skimping on details nor talking too much to cover up.

Also practice some lies of omission. *Don't* tell your man about something bad that happened at work or with a friend, even if you're dying to. That way, you will fall out of the habit of sharing everything with him so that crucial details won't slip out when you finally have your fling.

In addition, work on reducing your guilt reflex. Hide his lucky golf shirt on the morning of a game and then tell him, point blank, that you haven't seen it. Erase one of his favorite TV programs and explain that the TiVo must not have worked; depending on the show, this may make having an affair seem like no big deal. (But, please, no championship games. There's no reason to be cruel here!)

When you're lying to your loved one about having an affair, keep in mind that telling him the truth would be more catastrophic to his ego and detrimental to your relationship than "distorting" the truth or hiding the evidence. What you're doing by learning to lie is protecting what's most important to you—your man and your relationship—while satisfying some of your own needs or wants on the side.

Remember, what he doesn't know won't hurt him. So it's your duty as a loving wife or girlfriend to make sure he never finds out.

How to Hide the Money Trail

No matter what, an affair is going to cost you. At least financially, that is. Whether you're a man or a woman, there are expenses associated with committing adultery. Some of them may be as simple as paying for a hotel room or buying a pack of condoms (that's right, ladies—you can't always count on him to carry them). Others, which will we discuss in later chapters, involve investing in a second cell phone or purchasing a spare set of clothing.

Whether you had a one-time, out-of-town fling or more than one one-night stand, even the small costs can add up and attract your man's attention. That's why it's important to know how to hide the money trail.

The best advice is to always use cash for all of your expenses in order to eliminate evidence of your activities or purchases. This especially applies to out-of-town expenditures— another topic we will cover shortly—though the same "cash only" rule also goes for staying closer to home. If you do go out of town, don't make the mistake of paying for gas with a credit card; your significant other will take one look at your monthly statement and want to know what you were doing at a gas station so far away. He probably won't believe that they have the best unleaded, though he might start wondering whether you had gotten pumped.

It is quite possible that your spouse or significant other will notice some suspicious charges made to a hotel, bar, restaurant, lingerie store, etc. Even a small charge at a convenience store (for condoms, new pantyhose, coffee or even gum) can give you away if the date or time is at odds with the story you told him. Cold, hard money doesn't leave a paper trail. Therefore, it is imperative to cover your tracks by using cash for the following items and activities:

- Any extra or spare clothes

- Condoms

- Grooming items (shampoo, body spray, etc.)

- Hotel rooms

- Car rentals/gas

- Lunches and dinners

- Bars/night clubs

- Taxi rides

Cash withdrawals from your ATM/bank account must occur randomly and in a span of a few weeks before and after your fling in order to deter any possible attention. Each withdrawal should be made for different amounts to mask a pattern of behavior or any kind of ulterior agenda.

If you are the kind of person who charges even the smallest purchases (i.e., the kind of person I always seem to get behind in line), then start breaking that habit right away. Carry more cash on you, and make sure your partner sees you spend it, starting with smaller things. Tell him that you're concerned about identity theft and don't want to have to keep track of all of your purchases each time you use your credit card. Even practice your lying technique by explaining that this happened to a friend of yours recently when she used her card at a convenience store. That should satisfy his curiosity—and, as a bonus, he may even find your fiscal responsibility to be an irresistible turn-on!

Now I'm not saying that the woman should pay for the hotel room or buy drinks for her target at a bar. But, well… you never know. If you meet a young cub during a night out, he may not have enough cash to cover it, depending on when he got his last allowance. (I'm kidding, of course. If he's that young, you may want to move up in age bracket and experience.) Even if you meet an older man, he may not have cash on hand for a hotel room—and he may have his own reasons for not using his credit card. And that reason is probably waiting for him at home. So to be safe, ladies, have enough money with you to cover the unexpected. And if you do have to shell out, make sure you make him work for it later. You may not be able to put a price on love, but multiple orgasms should make up for some expenses.

The Gifts That Give You Away
(And No, It's Not Okay to Keep the Jewelry)

Part of hiding the evidence means you can't hold on to any mementos, reminders or tokens of your fling. No matter how great the sex was or how special he made you feel, you can't let your guard down by letting sentimentality creep in. When your time together is over, he literally needs to disappear without a trace. That means deleting any texts (even though they were sent to your disposable cell phone—more on this later) or emails (this is never a good idea, but if you have to have one, create a new account and then close it altogether at the end of the affair) that he sent you, no matter how sweet or whether it's something as simple as a smiley face; erasing any voice mail messages he left, even if you want to hear his voice again; throwing out his business card, even though you may want to keep in touch; and deleting his phone number from the contacts list on your disposable cell phone (even if you do have him saved as "Uncle Harry"). Overlooking these small reminders can lead to big trouble.

Ideally, if you follow the advice in the previous chapters, you'd know not to have any of his contact information or to have given him yours. You'd have an untraceable alias, and he couldn't reach you to leave a voice mail or email no matter how hard he tried. But I'm married, so believe me—I know that women don't always follow advice and usually wind up doing exactly what they want to do. For that reason, I also have to assume that some of my readers will break part of *Golden Rule #3* and sleep with the same man twice. Possibly even in the same night.

If that's the case, even more dangerous than a text or email are any kinds of gifts or tokens of affection that your fling may give you. Flowers sent to your office are like a ticking time bomb sitting on your desk, waiting to explode…except I imagine they smell better. All it takes is one coworker saying to your unsuspecting man at the next holiday party, "I wish my husband were as thoughtful as you," and your relationship could die before the roses do.

If your fling somehow does find out where you work and has flowers delivered to you, make sure you tell any inquiring minds that they were sent by a girlfriend whom you helped out recently with a relationship or personal problem. That should nip any rumors in the bud! Then take the flowers with you at the end of the day and deposit them in a convenient dumpster.

As for chocolates or candy, that's an easy one: eat the evidence! Whatever you can't personally consume on the ride home from seeing him, toss out. Do *not* take the box with you the next day to share with you coworkers. Do *not* smuggle any pieces of imported chocolate in your purse. Do *not* try hiding a truffle or two under your pillow. I know that many of you ladies are battling a serious addiction to chocolate, but the madness has to stop. For the sake of your relationship, rise above it and do the right thing!

You can always numb the pain the next day with some peanut M&Ms from your office vending machine.

Some well-meaning (and self-serving) flings may give you lingerie as a token of their esteem—or a hint that they like you to dress up like a high-class hooker. (Hey, save the hate mail! I said "high-class.") Even if you think you can sneak a small thong into your underwear drawer and wear it for your man someday, don't. First of all, that's just plain wrong, no matter how hot you look in it. Second of all, many of us men will notice a new addition to your repertoire, especially if it's not another pair of those broken-in cotton panties that we're so used to seeing (and have grown to love, I might add...at least for my own safety). Ditch the knickers if you get them as a gift.

Worst of all is the gift of jewelry. If your one-night stand turns into a full-blown affair that goes on for a few weeks or months—again, something that I strongly advise against—the other man might get the idea of giving you some bling to thank you for your fling. Though you most certainly deserve it, under no circumstances can you keep it. Even if it's as small as diamond stud earrings, your significant other will notice them simply because he didn't buy them for you (and, rest assured, he'll remember because he didn't spend hours wandering around the jewelry counter, looking lost and traumatized, and asking every saleswoman and female shopper, as well as calling up your mother and best friend, to see if they were something you would want).

I understand that jewelry is even more addictive than chocolate, but you've got to let it go. Do not pretend you bought it for yourself. Do not even try to give it to your best friend or sister, no matter how valuable it may be; no story will sound plausible to explain how or why you got it, even to the women closest to you. And don't even consider hawking it on eBay.

If possible, you can return it to the jewelry store and use the credit to pick out a nice pair of cufflinks for your man to surprise him on a special occasion—that is, if you have a strong enough stomach for it. If it was purchased at a department store, you can exchange it for clothing or cosmetics that you pick out for yourself (make sure your man sees you carrying the bags home, and tell him that you used cash since the department store credit cards charge ridiculous interest).

However, to get rid of the evidence entirely and any reminders of it, it's less risky to swing by a charity shop or community shelter and donate it for sale toward a good cause. Do this only if they accept anonymous donations, and make up a story about how the jewelry was a gift from your ex-husband that you don't want anymore since the divorce. After hearing that, they probably won't ask any more probing questions.

When it's all over, you can rest easy knowing that not only did you hide the evidence, protect your relationship and follow *Golden Rule #4*, but your affair actually helped make this world a better place. It's enough to make Mother Teresa proud! Well, almost.

Case Study #4

One Saturday morning, Jennifer took her eight-year-old son to his soccer game. To her delight she met the new coach, a genuine stud. He was great looking and in perfect shape—and you know what they say about soccer players: "They can do it for ninety minutes with only a ten-minute break."

Jen was all smiles as she was introduced to him. When they shook hands, it was instant attraction, or lust—whatever you want to call it. They couldn't take their eyes off of each other. Jen's husband was out of town and, after the game, the coach offered to get together with all the parents to discuss the team and their future plans.

The coach wanted to spend time getting to know Jen and used this gathering as a clever excuse. After the meeting was over, all the parents left—with the exception of Jen. Her son had left earlier with a neighbor, so she was all alone with the coach and was dying to learn new tricks about how to handle the ball!

Soon after that, they would meet an hour before each game on Saturdays since she volunteered to become the assistant coach. The chemistry between them was strong, and they both knew it was just matter of time before they got intimate. Weeks passed, and nothing happened until one Saturday after the game, when they finally decided that the urge was too overwhelming and arranged to meet in a hotel thirty miles outside of town.

They continued with this arrangement for weeks. On one occasion, they were supposed to meet at a hotel when the coach got stuck in traffic and Jen arrived on time. Since she did not want to wait in the lobby (for fear of being seen), she decided to get the hotel room herself and wait for him there. However, she wasn't thinking clearly and forgot that this action would leave a trace on her credit card statement.

Three weeks later, Jen's husband opened the mail and found the hotel charge. When he asked if it belonged to her, she emphatically denied it and volunteered to take care of the "mistake" immediately. Of course she didn't, but she told her husband that the charge was proven fraudulent and that the credit company had reversed it. Luckily, he never verified it.

Jen and the coach continued their secret rendezvous for weeks until she felt that he was becoming too attached. This was evident by the countless emails and text messages she was receiving. One day, she was reading her emails when the doorbell rang; it was her neighbor, and the two women got involved in conversation. Jen forgot that her email account was open. By accident, her husband saw that there were many messages from the same sender—someone he didn't recognize. It didn't take long for him to read through the graphic, erotic messages and figure out what was going on. Soon after, Jen got divorced for the second time. Game over.

Now let's see how Samantha followed *Golden Rule #4* when she took a new job that didn't require out-of-town trips—which she had come to consider a big employee perk.

Sam had always planned her affairs when she traveled on business trips; there were a lot fewer complications, and she was able to follow all **The 9 Golden Rules** requirements, which put her mind at ease that she would not be caught cheating on her husband.

Left with little choice now, she decided to develop a new schedule to establish solid patterns of behavior. To that end, although her job did not require long hours, she always stayed overtime. Her office was fifty-six miles away from her house, so she was certain her husband wouldn't make the drive to surprise her for lunch or any other reason.

She was also aware that he had a standing poker night on Wednesdays with his buddies that he would never miss. For Sam, the stage was set: any affair would be planned for Wednesdays, and coming home late was not an issue since she often deliberately stayed overtime at the office.

From time to time she would take a one-night trip out of town and pretend it was for business, just in case she had to resort to staying overnight with a lover in a hotel. Simply put, she covered all her bases for when the opportunity arose and she had to react.

Sam continued with this strategy for five months, and when she felt her husband was secure with her schedule and confident of her whereabouts, she pulled the trigger and planned an affair.

She knew the best place to meet strangers was in hotel bars, so she went to one downtown on a Wednesday evening after work. She sat at a table and ordered a drink; with her notebook computer opened, she pretended she was working and was not there to be hit on—in fact, far from it.

Within no time she got noticed by an out-of-town businessman who asked if he could join her. The two hit it off and spent the next couple of hours getting to know each other. When he asked her if she would like to continue the conversation in his room, she accepted, and the two made love.

Noting the time, Sam knew she had to leave when out of the blue the generous businessman offered her an unopened bottle of expensive champagne to take home with her. She accepted graciously, and they parted ways.

As soon as she got to the parking garage, she discarded the champagne without hesitation or regret, knowing that as tempting as it was, it would be against *Golden Rule #4* to take the bottle home. After all, how could she explain it to her husband?

Due to her clear thinking, precise planning and level-headedness, Sam was able to enjoy a successful one-night stand—as well as a champagne toast with her husband on their following anniversary.

GOLDEN RULE #5

Get out of Town

Golden Rule #5 **explains** why it's a good idea to keep your distance—and I don't just mean that emotionally. When it comes to having flings, the more far-flung the better. We're talking earning serious airline points with each affair! Take it on the road, "get down to business" on business trips, "get down" out of town…but whatever you do, keep your extracurricular activities *away from home*.

The "69" Rule

The "69 Rule" is an easy one to remember—for obvious reasons. But no matter what your preferred position is, try to engage in it at least sixty-nine miles away from your house. That means making the best use of your business trips, family visits and out-of-town sporting or social events (for example, high school reunions or college friends' weddings…you know, the kind of things your significant other would rather *not* attend—that way, you're sort of doing him a favor).

The 69 Rule is perhaps one of the most vital of all, and it comes with many built-in advantages, such as:

- ☞ Few people know who you are.

- ☞ The probability of your spouse or boyfriend seeing you with someone else is minimal.

- ☞ The chance that one of your significant other's friends or associates will see you with someone else is minimal.

- ☞ The likelihood of your colleagues (who know your significant other) seeing you with someone else is minimal.

- ☞ You can act and behave like a single woman.

- ☞ You can be whoever you want to be by creating your own identity and fantasy.

- ☞ There is no time restriction (i.e., having to be home by dinner time).

- ☞ Once you leave that town, everything about the affair is forgotten and vanishes.

- ☞ There is no evidence of your infidelity.

☞ Entrapment is less of a possibility.

☞ Being pursued or stalked is less of a probability.

When you commit adultery out of town with advance preparation and a predetermined false identity, you become a new woman—one who has no ties or history to what you left behind. For a few days, at least.

This is the reason women who are well-disciplined and possess strong will power commit infidelity while they are far away from home: they know their chances of getting caught are practically negligible. Once the trip has ended, they leave with only a great memory…and no extra baggage!

However, as we've seen, cheating on your spouse or significant other is always somewhat of a risky adventure, and this book has taught you that caution should be exercised in all aspects of your affairs. For example, one risky element to note is the type of men you could meet on the road. Of course it is difficult, in a very short span of time, to determine the state of mind or the psychological characteristics of a man you just met on an out-of-town trip. Nevertheless, it's up to you to examine your options and carefully make a selection.

As a married/involved woman, you must always assume the worst-case scenario, which is that the man with whom you are about to have casual sex will want more and will try to pursue you further. Carrying on away from home will make this situation much less likely, but you should still try to figure out what you're up against. As a general guide, here are a few types of men you may meet on the road:

☞ Single with no ties

☞ Married on a business trip

- Obsessed with finding the "right" girl and getting married

- Looking only for sex

- Looking for something more substantial

- Insecure and needing to "prove" his manhood

- An evil one

- A party boy

- A player

- A psycho

- A young cub looking for experience

- The jealous type

The first two types are among the best choices since they are out to have a good time, engage in conversation and perhaps spend an otherwise lonely night with someone of equal quality and with similar needs. A single man with no ties might be a "career guy" who is too busy with his professional goals and is not the type who would pursue you when you try to break ties (as you should). The second type is also a suitable selection since he is married and wishes to get back to his life (and wife) in a few days; it's a certainty that he would leave you alone after the affair, especially if you used a false identity.

The other ones can sometimes be wild cards. Any man obsessed with marriage, looking for a substantial relationship or too insecure could easily turn out to be the clingy type who doesn't want to let you go so easily. A guy looking only for sex, a party boy or a player might give you a good time for a few short minutes, but he may not be good for a full one-night stand, and he'll probably act as though he's rocked your world afterward. He may be easy to ditch, but do you really want to put up with that?

The young cub and the jealous type might work much harder at finding you after your fling, so you might want to give them a pass unless you've really done your preparation to hide your identity. As for the evil guy and the psycho, well...really, their descriptions say everything you need to know. Avoid them like you'd avoid the plastic surgeons of the *Beverly Hills Housewives.*

In short, be vigilant, sharpen your interpersonal skills (and your antennae) and discover as much as you can about your potential target to determine if he's the most suitable man for the job—at least for the night. Then trust your judgment and pursue your goal.

However, if you fail to make the right selection regarding your casual sex partner, the advantage of committing adultery far away from home is that it significantly reduces his ability to pursue, entrap or stalk you—as long as you used a fake identity. That way, everything he knows about you is false, such as:

☞ Your name

☞ Your cell phone number

☞ Your job

☞ Your hometown/birthplace

☞ Your age (but, of course, all women lie about that one!)

☞ Which high school and university you attended (even where you spent spring breaks)

☞ Who your friends are

☞ Which towns you visit for your job

As we learned in *Golden Rule #1*, it's essential to create a new identity: be creative and stylish in developing an imaginary you, from your profession all the way to the names of your friends and relatives. Don't get lazy, comfortable or careless just because you're out of town! Remember, any *true* information can still be traced back to you, no matter how far away you live. Google searches and people-finder web sites have made the world a much smaller place and have taken a lot of the anonymity out of adultery.

If you follow all of the above elements of the 69 Rule, it will put you in the perfect *position* to carry out an affair with success and without the fear of getting caught.

Checklists for Out-of-Town Trips

Prior to your trip away from home, you must develop a preparation checklist to ensure that all necessary items are organized and available for utilization as planned or in case of any contingencies. Here are few things you must think about and include on your list:

☞ Make a cash withdrawal so you don't leave a credit card trail.

☞ Purchase a prepaid cell phone so there aren't any phone records to trace.

☞ If possible, purchase a fake ID.

☞ Purchase a business card software program and print your own (false, of course) cards.

☞ Store all of the above items at work, or somewhere safe (except the cash).

☞ Keep your checklist at work, or somewhere safe, and discard it before your departure.

Cash withdrawals

Obtain sufficient cash from your bank account in a span of a few weeks, using multiple-denomination withdrawals to conceal a pattern. Make sure you have enough funds for an additional hotel room, entertainment, dinners/drinks, clothing and other incidentals while you are on your trip.

Purchase a prepaid cell phone

Purchase a prepaid and disposable cell phone from Walmart, Target, Kmart or other leading superstores. The benefits of using such a phone will be discussed in greater detail under *Golden Rule #6*.

Purchase a fake ID card

You can purchase a fake driver's license or other identification cards from Internet sites, but be careful of scams. The really authentic-looking ones will accept only cash sent in an envelope to a prescribed location, often out of the country. If, for obvious reasons, you're not willing to send $160 to a stranger in China, Canada or the UK for an illegal item, consider one of the cheaper "novelty card" web sites or even stores in immigrant communities in most metropolitan cities. These probably won't fool a discerning bouncer or bartender, but they should do the trick if you flash it quickly before your intended fling's eyes. In one glance he'll get all the information you want him to believe about you.

Purchase business card software
(and print your own cards)

You should purchase a business card software program such as "My Professional Business Cards," "Business Card Composer" or "Business Card Shop" from one of the leading electronics superstores, such as Best Buys, Fry's or CompUSA. The price varies depending on the complexity and sophistication of the software.

While you're out, buy business card paper from leading office supply stores such as Staples, Office Depot, etc. Then you're ready to use the purchased software program to develop business cards that match your desired false identity. Print and store the cards at work, alongside other trip essentials, and remember that these purchases must be done at the store (not online) and using cash only. You should discard the receipts upon exiting the store to eliminate any evidence and delete all computer files pertaining to these business cards once you've printed them out.

Keep the checklist at work

Store your checklist at work (or somewhere safe) for reference, and cross out each entry as you proceed. Once you're done, discard the list. Now might be as good a time as any to finally learn how to use your office paper shredder!

Of course, you'll have to make another checklist for things you need while you're away. To look more attractive and desirable (and less "married" or "involved"), certain modifications and alterations to your appearance might be necessary. However, these changes must take place while you are on your trip or away from home in order to avoid suspicion. When you arrive at your destination, the first thing to do is to purchase:

- ☞ two pairs of sexy underwear

- ☞ one sexy outfit

- ☞ a small bottle of sexy perfume

- ☞ okay, these next two are not so sexy: unscented shampoo and body wash (more about this in *Golden Rule #7*)

- ☞ condoms

- ☞ souvenirs for your kids (if you have any kids, and if you are on a trip)

- ☞ a souvenir for your significant other—*only if* you have always purchased one for him in the past when you traveled. Now is *not* the time to break any habits!

The advantage of buying the clothing and perfume out of town is that your companion will remain unaware of your motives or agenda; at the same time, you will be able to dress up and disguise yourself as a single woman. The unscented shampoo and body wash are to hide any trace of smoke or strange cologne while not arousing suspicion that you're trying too hard to cover up or that you showered just before coming home. The condoms, of course, are for just in case he's not packing. And the souvenirs are a nice touch to show you were thinking of your loved one(s) while you were away.

Once again, you will have to make a last list before your departure back home to make sure you've discarded all evidence of your infidelity. Remind yourself to:

- ☞ Discard your two new undergarments and perfume.

- ☞ Discard your new outfit as a precaution in case you picked up any cologne scent or stray hairs during your entanglement.

- ☞ Discard your unscented shampoo or body wash.

- ☞ Discard any extra business cards and condoms.

- ☞ Discard your prepaid cell phone.

- ☞ Hide your fake ID.

- ☞ Place the souvenirs in your carry-on underneath any convention, business trip or other travel-related materials, such as catalogues or brochures.

- ☞ Discard all checklists.

With some preparation and everything in place, you should be free and clear to enjoy your "hunting" trip.

An Eye on the Odometer

For those of you following the 69 Rule and driving out of town for one-day "excursions," don't kid yourself: he does keep track of the odometer.

Keep in mind that most men are obsessed with cars, down to checking the mileage. If you have your affairs out of town, which, again, is highly recommended for the sake of anonymity, make sure you can explain your recent increase in long drives. Plan ahead so you don't get caught unprepared. Or caught *period*.

Excuses for Those Awkward Encounters

Even if you're out of town and think you're in the clear, you may run into an acquaintance. It must be pointed out here that in most infidelity cases, the partner learns of improper behavior through a witness: a neighbor, co-worker, family member, friend, friend's wife…the list of potential private dicks is endless. Similar to any other crime, the witness plays an important role in convicting you of infidelity because it is difficult to deny and refute the witness's discovery. To this end you must avoid exposure at any cost, even when you're away.

If your partner knows you're staying at a Hilton, try the Marriott's bar instead. If you usually hate beer, you might want to prowl the local microbrewery rather than a wine bar, if that's your usual choice. If you can't stand football, keep in mind that a sports bar is a great place to meet men, especially on game night. Then, on the off-chance that someone does spot you, it will be a lot easier to dispute their story since your partner knows your habits, likes and dislikes.

If you do run face-to-face into someone you and your partner know, keep your cool and lie your head off. If you're on a business trip, introduce your new friend as a colleague. If you're at a family reunion, pass him off as a second cousin. Keep your story in line with your reason for being out of town and you're more than halfway home to believability!

If you follow all the guidelines in this chapter, by the time you leave town and head back home, all evidence of your infidelity will be discarded, removed and no longer in existence. No, I'm not saying you should whack your one-night stand when you're done with him, á la Tony Soprano or any other wise guy, but definitely do be a wise girl. Keep your identity to yourself, even when you're in a new place, and conduct your personal affairs far from your own front stoop. *Capeesh*?

Case Study #5

One afternoon, Jennifer went to the local grocery store to buy some milk for her boyfriend's breakfast. When she entered the store, she noticed a dark-haired, handsome man in the produce section.

Instead of going to the dairy section, Jen changed her route to get a closer look at this specimen in the produce aisle. In a split second her lust and curiosity manipulated her behavior, and her hormones got the better of her; in short, she lost her self-control.

Pretending to shop for fruit, Jen got close to the man and initiated a conversation with him. He acknowledged her, smiled and returned her greeting.

Encouraged by his reaction, Jen remained engaged in a conversation with him for a few more minutes when she suddenly saw Peter, a friend of her boyfriend, entering the store. Jen suddenly realized she was there to pick up a gallon of milk, not a gym guy with a nice face and perfect physique. Her sudden return to reality and awareness was as if someone had shocked her with an electrical current. This was indeed something of a miracle since Jen had never believed in self-control, discipline and/or planning and hardly ever complied with or used The 9 Golden Rules in her affairs. As a result, her lack of success has been demonstrated by her failed marriages.

Anyway, she immediately selected a few oranges and left the area without saying another word to the guy. Needless to say, he was surprised and disappointed by her sudden departure, but he didn't pursue Jen.

There were two opposite and significant events that took place within this incident, and both had to do with self-control. Jen's initial reaction to the target of her desire as she entered the store could be considered a complete loss of self-control. She operated on pure instinct, without a plan or objective, even though she wasn't prepared to carry through with a fling at that time.

The second event that took place was solely based on her fear of the unknown, the proximity to her home and the fact that she had learned some lessons from her failed affairs in the past. By immediately breaking the connection and departing abruptly, perhaps for the first time she demonstrated unusual self-control by removing herself from the environment and any further temptation.

It's important to note that Jen had dropped by her *local* grocery store—nowhere near sixty-nine miles from her home. What would have happened if she had continued her conversation with the fitness buff and somehow Peter had seen her, and this leaked back to her boyfriend? For certain she would have drawn attention to herself. She would have been viewed with suspicion as someone who was playing the field or entertaining thoughts of cheating. All it takes is a rumor or one inappropriate move to draw unwanted attention and destroy the trust of your companion, not to mention a relationship.

As you can see, a simple error in judgment or her usual loss of self-control could have been disastrous for Jen. Luckily, she realized just in time that what she was doing was inappropriate and risky, and she finally displayed enough strength and self-discipline to save herself from the inherent danger of exposure, especially so close to home.

Compare this incident to the time when Samantha went on a business trip to Ohio. For a few months in advance she had planned on and organized for an opportunity for infidelity.

During the first day of the convention, she met a man from Nebraska, who was also there on business but for an entirely separate matter. Knowing they had no one in common, Sam introduced herself as Diane, a saleswoman from the immediate area, with which she was familiar from previous business trips. After an hour chatting and laughing with her newfound friend, Sam sensed there was some chemistry and an opportunity to get intimate. She knew all the loose ends were tied up and all the pieces of her plan were in place to proceed, so all she had to do was execute it.

The significance of Sam's affair was that she carried out her plan to perfection. She did not alter any details, she did not reveal or take any chances exposing her true identity, and she did not allow herself to get overexcited or carried away. In her mind she treated the sexual encounter as a one-time event that had nothing to do with her real life back home; more important, she did not bring the affair back with her by fantasizing about it days later.

Suppose Sam had enjoyed the sex and their time together so much that, in an attempt to see him again, she had confessed her true identity before her departure. That would have meant that her emotions had taken over even though her plan was designed to prevent her from such a trap or disclosure.

The very reason you plan an activity is to ensure that, in the heat of the moment, when judgment might be clouded, you do not take actions that have not been previously considered for their consequences. In simple terms, a plan is in place just in case you cannot trust yourself to make good decisions at the critical time. Sam was able to meet her objective and enjoy her encounter because she had all the tools necessary to succeed and the peace of mind to know that her actions wouldn't come back to haunt her. She had waited for the right time and, more important, the right place: more than two thousand miles from her home.

Sam's fling may have thought that fate had brought them together. Only Sam herself knew that their one night of bliss was the result of weeks of preparation and miles of distance between them.

GOLDEN RULE

#6

Cut the Talk

This rule will teach you how to stay in communication—and in control.

A lot of affairs are discovered due to careless communication; undeleted emails, texts and voicemail messages can definitely come back to haunt you. Sure, it's only natural to want to save that text that says, "U were amazing last nite" or "U rocked my world," but saving such an ego boost is not worth the possibility of its being discovered. That's why they invented the "erase" button on cell phones. Use it.

Of course, overall, I don't suggest staying in touch with the object of your one-night stand. But I understand that plans must be made, rendezvous set up and times for trysts scheduled. Other than the essentials, try to cut the talk. You don't need a post-game wrap-up or play-by-play analysis and, believe me, he can live without the smiley face emoticon you're tempted to send him. The smile on his face says it all.

Prepaid Cell Phones Are a Girl's Best Friend

We've already touched on the risks associated with giving him your real cell phone number, work number or email address. Remember the false identity and fake business cards? Basically, those are to protect you from any kind of phone records, text records or email trails.

But there are times when you may need to get in touch (though you should really refrain from drunk texting or last-minute booty calls, no matter how good an idea it seems as the time; so did that last margarita, remember?). So a girl's best option is often a prepaid cell phone. Don't you just love disposable technology?

These handy devices can be purchased from Walmart, Target, Kmart or any other of the leading superstores. Here are the benefits of using a prepaid cell phone:

☞ They are not traceable.

☞ No billing statement comes to your home or P.O. Box.

☞ They are small and discreet. Hide it in your purse, and your significant other never has to know about it.

There are five important points to remember regarding prepaid cell phones:

☞ You cannot use it for any other personal purposes, such as calling your:

  ☞ Husband/boyfriend

  ☞ Children

  ☞ Parents

  ☞ Friends

  ☞ Associates or anyone you know in your hometown

It is for *affairs* only.

You must purchase this product at the store using cash only. *Do not* order it online since you will leave a trace in the form of an order confirmation email or a credit card statement.

It is crucial to discard the receipt of the prepaid cell phone immediately after leaving the store.

☞ Store the cell phone or the SIM card in your office, or somewhere else safe, alongside other accessories for out-of-town trips. If you have to carry it with you, make sure to turn it off (or have the SIM card removed) when you're at home.

☞ Dispose of the cell phone and SIM card after the affair is over. If you used it for an out-of-town fling during a business trip, etc., discard them before coming back. The farther away from home, the better.

Even with a second cell phone, make sure to erase all evidence of incriminating messages, calls made/received and texts as soon as you get them. You can always explain away having an extra phone (for example by saying it's for certain emergency clients at work), but it's much more difficult to explain sexting or pictures of penises saved in your photo messages!

In fact, the conservative approach is to discard the prepaid cell phone once the affair is done to ensure that no trace is left behind. That way, you won't have to worry about getting caught with an extra phone. After all, it might be a while before you start another affair, so don't take a chance. Be a coward, but live to cheat again.

As has the Internet, cell phones have made infidelity so much easier and less traceable. (Some people say that as if it's a bad thing!) But the trick is to exercise common sense and self-control. If you must let your fingers do the walking, save it for the bed in the hotel room and not your BlackBerry.

Just Business—Nothing Personal

Fielding phone calls at work from your fling is always tricky business. For one thing, office gossip is still a faster form of communication than email or even IM, so you don't want any coworkers overhearing your conversation, especially one that involves the phrase "You know that motel near the freeway where the hookers hang out?" or "Don't forget to bring the lube."

Second, once the affair is over, it's best that he doesn't have an actual place at which to contact you—particularly at your desk with your boss standing over you, wondering why you're not answering the phone.

As we discussed earlier in the creation of a false identity, one convincing factor is a business card on which the contact information can be shared with your fling or target. To make this easier, there are four methods of handling the issue of a business phone number; your choice depends primarily on the level of sophistication you want to achieve and your willingness to take extra risks.

Method 1
Do not show him your business card

Advantage: Your work phone number usually appears on your business card, but seldom do men ask women for their cards or use them for personal reasons. However, if a target does ask you for a business card, simply state that you ran out or you don't carry yours. Using this method, there is no need to create or exchange a business phone number where you can be reached.

Disadvantage: He might feel you are hiding something from him or avoiding the truth. And he might ask you straight out for your work number even if you don't have a business card.

Method 2
Do not provide your work phone number on the business card

Advantage: Some modern business cards provide only a cell phone number or company website as the contact information. If you have these kinds of cards made up, there is no need to create or worry about a business phone number.

Disadvantage: For the older-age group and some certain professions, this might look unprofessional or dubious. Plus, you should make sure it's not your real cell phone number.

Method 3
Use a virtual phone service

Advantage: Virtual telephone services provide a live operator to answer your dedicated phone line per your scripted greetings. It sounds as if someone is working out of your own office, so it is highly believable. The monthly fee for such services runs between $14.99 and $29.99.

You may also choose to have a recording answer your business phone line. The monthly fee for such a service is under $10. You can check the web using search words such as "virtual telephone services" to get prices and additional information.

Disadvantage: It is traceable. Let's assume, under a worst-case scenario, that one of your one-night stands wishes to see you again because he thinks you are a great catch or wants to blackmail you into seeing him by threatening to expose the affair. A reputable investigator can trace your phone number back to the virtual telephone service company, which, in turn, can release your personal information.

You are exposed because, at the signing of the contract, you provided personal information such as a driver's license, social security number and valid credit card.

Method 4
Purchase a second prepaid cell phone (recommended)

Advantage: The most foolproof and recommended approach is to purchase a second prepaid cell phone and designate it as your business phone number. You can record your own message to sound as if your one-night stand has reached your personal line at work. Be sure to dispose of it after your affair, just as you did with the other disposable cell phone.

Disadvantage: The cost of purchasing the second prepaid cell phone.

> ☞ Along with your work phone number, you
> also want to be careful with your business
> email address or web site. This is usually an
> easier matter since you can give out that
> falsified information without much risk or
> chance of immediate discovery—unless the
> guy whips out his SmartPhone and punches
> it in on the spot. Then you might want to
> use the GPS on your SmartPhone to find
> the nearest possible exit. Either way, though,
> the presence of an email address or web site
> on your card makes it appear more complete
> and legitimate, so you may want to consider
> the following methods.

Email address

I do not recommend that you provide a valid email address on your card. Instead, create a false "yahoo.com" or "gmail.com" address and display it on a card that you have made up. Of course, you can also open another email account strictly to manage your "affairs," but since the idea is to not have any contact with your one-night stands after the deed, providing an accurate email address of any kind is highly discouraged.

Web page

I strongly advise against providing a web address on your business card. Even if there is no specific information about you on the site, it's amazing what a little persistence can turn up—and, believe me, a lot of these guys will be persistent; no matter how much we men say they want just a "one-night stand," when it comes to casual sex, we'd much rather turn it into two or three nights…or weeks…or months, for that matter. One call to customer service and he may find your work extension, email address or entire life story.

House Calls

I don't care if he is a doctor—house calls are a no-no. Under absolutely no circumstance is it ever advisable to let your target know your home phone number or to call him from the landline in your house. However, with all the people search web sites out there that reveal your address as well as your private number, it's always a possibility that you'll receive an unexpected call in the middle of the night— or your significant other will start experiencing a whole lot of hang-ups. (Web searches are one reason not to reveal your true name since other information is sure to follow.)

If you *do* get that dreaded house call, don't panic. Stay cordial and even-toned and explain that you'll call him back later (and do so from your prepaid cell phone). You will have to make up a believable caller to appease your significant other—and a good reason to explain to your new friend *never* to call that number again (a good one is that you keep the line open for emergency calls from your parents; another good one is that you're married or in a serious relationship. At that point, the truth can't hurt, right?).

If you do decide to have an affair, you may seriously want to consider getting rid of your landline altogether (no one really needs one anymore, plus you can convince your significant other that it's a good way to save some money).

When it comes to infidelity, it's better to take action…and cut the talk.

Remaining Textually Active

Do not let technology trip you up. Texts and emails are forever, even though flings aren't. Whatever you send the guy—and the raunchier it is, the truer this is—he may save on his phone or forward to ten friends, who will forward it to ten more. It's like a venereal disease that keeps getting passed on. So, to stop the spread of "textually transmitted disease," I bring you this brief guide of what not to say, send or snap a photo of:

- ☞ Nothing about "last nite" or anything else that can place you together at any specific time

- ☞ Nothing that explicitly makes it clear that you had sex (that includes any expressions heard in rap songs)

- ☞ No terms of endearment ("baby" is bad; "tiger" and "stud puppet" are worse)

- ☞ No pictures of private parts (you may be identifiable by a small mole you never knew you had)

- ☞ No pictures of your face

- ☞ No pictures of the two of you together

In fact, no pictures of you at all unless you're wearing full-body armor…and, really, how sexy can that be? Okay, maybe a little sexy. Make that *loose-fitting* full-body armor.

If you're going to remain in touch (which may be human nature but is against **The 9 Golden Rules**) via text or email, keep it as neutral or even businesslike as possible ("When can you meet, as we discussed?") and then erase all texts as soon as you read them and even the messages from your secondary email account. Don't get sentimental and save sweet texts; they can be the honey traps that get you caught. Also, don't get horny and send sexy texts that you'll later regret. Remember, your phone is for necessary communication, not foreplay. Unless, of course, you keep it on vibrate.

Case Study #6

It was 10:00 a.m. the morning after Samantha got back into town from her two-day business trip. On the trip she had had a great time with a young man from Denver.

As she was drinking her coffee in her office and following her post-trip routine (making sure all evidence of her infidelity was discarded), she discovered that she had not disposed of the prepaid cell phone she had used. Although the cell phone was turned off and there was no danger of receiving calls, she quickly removed the SIM card and trashed it (she always destroyed the SIM card to make sure no data could be recovered if it accidentally got into the wrong hands). But as soon as she picked up the cell phone to do the same, her boss walked in.

She stopped on the spot. It was too late to do anything now since it would have looked very suspicious to throw out a brand-new cell phone in his presence, so she placed the phone in her purse with the intention of discarding it at a later time when her boss—or anyone else for that matter—wasn't around.

Sam got busy at work and lost track of what she had to do regarding her routine. At the end of the day she went home and suddenly remembered that the phone was still in her possession. She knew she had to get rid of it immediately, so she did.

Later, when her husband was sorting out the recycling for trash pickup, he noticed a brand-new cell phone in the bin. He thought perhaps this was done by mistake and asked Sam.

She was initially surprised by her husband's discovery, but as a trained and successful cheater, she came up with a great explanation on the spot:

"The company provided us with this new trial cell phone to track our movements and expenses while on trips. But it seems an agreement wasn't reached between our company and the cell phone carrier, so they came to our offices and requested the SIM cards back. Since I have no need for a second cell phone, I trashed it. Anyone who wants to contact me can reach me using my regular cell phone. Do you want it?" she asked her husband.

He replied, "No; I have no use for it either."

Sam was ever so convincing. Note that she did not use the old cliché, "This isn't mine...It belongs to my best friend," or any other not very convincing or common excuse that we men can always see through and never believe.

Sure, Sam made a mistake; she should have thrown away the prepaid cell phone before she had gone home. If she had followed The 9 Golden Rules guidelines, she would have never been caught in this scenario in the first place. Luckily, she had the presence of mind to remove the SIM card—the "smoking gun"—from the phone as soon as she saw it, so even with the discovery, there was no way for her to be trapped or her affair uncovered.

Now, compare this incident to when Jennifer decided, once again, that rules and guidelines are too much of burden to follow and comply with. Jen, who had had a one-night stand with an out-of-town salesman a couple of weeks earlier, suddenly received a text from him saying he'd be in town again in two days.

Since Jen had used her own identity and had given the guy her real cell phone number, it was quite easy for him to find her and want to rekindle that magical night. The two exchanged many texts before he arrived in town. As the texts were getting more and more graphic and hotter in nature and content, Jen looked forward to receiving them and seeing him again. In the excitement of the anticipated affair, she ignored The 9 Golden Rules of engagement.

At the time, Jen's third husband was out of town visiting his friend and was also texting her on occasion, updating her on what he was doing and engaging in small talk. Jen received a text from her lover while she was driving home; the message got her juices going, and her emotions took over. That is when she made the dreadful mistake.

She replied to his text, describing in detail some of the sexual acts they performed and what he should expect at the King's Hotel on Wednesday night. Unfortunately, she replied to the wrong man. It was her husband who received the text.

Jen's husband did not reply but cut his trip short to return home the next day—and his destination was the King's Hotel. He waited in the lobby, and as Jen walked in expecting to see the salesman, he confronted her there and then.

Instead of following *Golden Rule #6* and cutting the talk, Jen learned the hard way when her husband cut her loose.

#7

Don't Change Your Personal Habits
(But Do Change Your Panties)

This chapter will explore ways to help you keep up appearances without alerting suspicion. Now, let's face it: most women don't need as much assistance in this department as men do. When men enter into a monogamous relationship or marriage, we tend to, uh, let ourselves go a little. We've already got the girl, so we're officially off the market. Surely she doesn't care if we go up a pant size or two. If she wanted sexy, she would've married George Clooney, right?

Women, on the other hand, keep working at it. They want their significant other to still find them desirable. They want other women to envy them. They don't mind a little extra attention from other men now and then. And, well, they can always keep the option open of having an affair if their significant other lets himself go a little too significantly.

Still, there are some personal habits or grooming techniques that women may need to consider when a new target comes along. And so while, for personal reasons, I may be tempted to tell each and every female reader out there to buy and wear thongs as often as possible, for professional purposes I feel compelled to point out that you should not change your habits or appearance too drastically when planning an affair.

Here Comes the "Groom"

Let's say your man doesn't mind the "peach fuzz" effect going on down under. Hell, he's happy to be getting some and won't let a day or two of your skipping shaving deter him. In fact, he's totally used to it—and to the stubble burn. How then are you going to explain your brand-new Brazilian wax coming out of the blue?

The answer is, once again, planning. When you decide that you're going to start the process of finding a fling, you have to introduce any changes in your appearance early on. When you come home with the full Brazilian, explain to your man (after you resuscitate him from the pleasant but heart-stopping shock) that you wanted to try something new to surprise him and add a little spice to your love life. Most men are gullible—and eager—enough to buy this. And why not, if you have the foresight to implement these changes at least a month before engaging in any act of infidelity? Nothing will seem suspicious, your behavior and habits will be the same and your significant other will be too eternally grateful to ruin it all by asking any questions.

This goes for working out/toning up, changing your hair and buying sexier clothes or lingerie. And as for feeling guilty, think of it this way: you may be doing it to attract higher-quality targets once you're in the market for an affair, but your significant other is the one who'll be benefiting the most!

The point is to avoid changing your habits, tastes and tendencies too soon before committing adultery because these can be loud signals that you are either planning or having an affair. Men know that single women act, talk and dress differently than those who are married or involved. For example, a married woman would dress more conservatively most of the time, but when she changes this habit and buys sexier outfits, she is sending a message that something has changed.

For this reason you should plan your changes or purchases well in advance if indeed you wish to alter your habits, tastes, tendencies or appearance in any noticeable way. Some women even wait as long as three or four months after changing their image before committing adultery because they know very well that their husband or boyfriend will be monitoring them closely during this period due to these changes.

The following are some of the routines and personal habits that are being monitored by your significant other whether you realize it or not. Pay close attention if you are planning to make any changes in:

☞ type of clothing

☞ style of underwear

☞ hairstyle (that goes for all hair on your body)

☞ exercise

Of course, the easier route is to make changes to your style of clothing and makeup only when you are on a business trip or out of town (as discussed in the *Golden Rule #5*) to avoid any suspicion on the part of your significant other. Before returning home, discard all the items you purchased for the occasion and resume the same habits, style and tendencies you had before as if nothing has changed. You'll have had your fun, and your man will be happy to have you back, sweats, stubbly legs and all.

Of Showers and Spare Clothes

Okay, ladies, here's a topic dear to my heart that I'd like to address…in as much detail as possible. Hint: it involves you getting sudsy in the shower.

You must shower after you had casual sex with a stranger to remove any scent or evidence that may have been transferred onto you or your clothing during intimacy. However, it's not as simple as that.

Even though taking a shower is a normal act that most individuals perform daily, its timing might raise some suspicions. For example, suppose you were on a business trip, had sex in the late afternoon and took a shower before your departure. When you arrive home at around 9:30 p.m., your man expects to find you tired and a bit untidy, not neat, groomed and ready for your close-up. In this case, your too-perfect appearance might cause alarm.

If you had a sexual encounter the day before you returned home, then you don't need to take any additional action and should follow your normal shower routine. However, if you had an encounter on the same day as your flight home, or you had an affair in town close to home, then you must take certain precautions to avoid any suspicion.

To prepare for these two scenarios, you must always carry a small bottle of unscented shampoo and body wash as part of your preparations. The advantage of organic, unscented shampoos and soaps are that they clean thoroughly but do not leave any fragrance that would indicate that you recently got out of the shower. Do not use any additional perfume, body spray or deodorant.

To make it even more realistic, you must exert some energy after the shower while wearing your clothes in order to generate enough sweat (or, for you ladies who don't sweat, enough of a "dewy glow") to create the impression that you took a shower much earlier in the day and not just a few minutes before coming home. Upon arriving home, after spending some time with your man, you may even want to take another shower to create the appearance of freshening up in order to get ready for bed or possible intimacy.

Also, to avoid any evidence of rumpled clothes or lingering cologne, make sure you bring along an appropriate change of clothing—including, of course, panties (put them in your gym bag, your briefcase or a handbag big enough to hide everything). Either dispose of your original clothing or get it into the washing machine with the rest of the load immediately upon returning home. (If you never do laundry at that time, don't risk it; it's better to just dump the clothes...besides, it'll give you a good reason to go shopping.) Get rid of the panties either way, especially if they're new or if your significant other hasn't had the pleasure of seeing them for some time.

Do not hide a change of clothing or your used clothes in your trunk; you never know when your man will go rummaging around in there in search of jumper cables or to change the batteries in your roadside-assistance flashlight. While that may be a good reason to keep him around, he won't be around for long if he discovers your secret stash.

The Scent of a Woman

A lot of women try to skip the showering/spare clothes rule and just cover up their "crime" with copious amounts of perfume or body spray. How much body spray is a dead giveaway? Let me put it like this: coming home smelling like you work in a bordello (or worse, in the perfume aisle of a major department store) isn't exactly going to go unnoticed. There's nothing subtle about this tactic. In fact, you'd raise less suspicion wearing a neon sign around your neck that read, "I Just Had An Affair."

Trying to cover up the smell of sex or the scent of another man's cologne on you with more perfume is like trying to hide an elephant in the room by placing a bigger elephant in front of it. Do yourself and everyone in the elevator with you a favor: skip the olfactory overload and stick with the quick shower using unscented shampoo/body wash instead. What your man can't smell he won't question.

Protect Yourself

This one should practically go without saying, but it's easy to make mistakes in the heat of the moment. That's why it's essential for women who are planning to have an affair to carry protection—and I don't mean mace. Even though it's usually the man's job, you ladies should bring along condoms just in case he's either too stupid or is caught unprepared (remember: you're the one who was doing the planning; he's just going along for the ride).

Regardless of how well you disguised your affairs, all it takes is something harder to disguise, such as a venereal disease or a pregnancy, to reveal your infidelity to your husband or boyfriend. But there's another reason that this section about condoms comes in a chapter about grooming: latex has a definite and discernible scent. If you don't have a) a rubber, and b) access to a shower, don't have sex.

Effective Affections

This final section on personal habits has less to do with the physical and more to do with the emotional. When you're planning on having an affair, it's essential to show your significant other the same level of affection to which he is accustomed. I'm sorry to say that means if the poor guy wasn't getting much action before, he shouldn't be getting any more now. (Don't get me wrong; all guys would be grateful, but some would also be suspicious.) Conversely, if your man is lucky enough to get a lot of sexual attention from you, there's no going cold turkey once you get involved with someone else.

You should continue to demonstrate to your spouse or boyfriend how much you love and care for him, making him believe he is the only one in your life. Once he feels secure, you are free to proceed with your infidelities.

As time passes and the routine of daily life settles in, we tend to forget that we must provide nutrition for the love we have for our companion. We tend to stop telling them how much we love, need and want them since we think that constant reaffirmation of these facts is not required.

On the contrary, if you plan to cheat on your man, do not stop telling him how much you love him, how amazing he looks (even with the extra few pounds) and, most of all, how much he turns you on sexually. Even though the feeling may be fading, keep up and display your regular desire for sex. This provides the impression that he is still desirable and attractive to you, and that is all he needs to feel comfortable and safe in your relationship rather than becoming suspicious of your activities.

To this end, as you begin the process of cheating on your man, you must maintain a steady pattern of desire, love and affection for him. Don't overdo it to the point that he's suddenly looking at you like you're a Stepford Wife or wondering where you learned the reverse cowgirl, but make sure you keep doing the little things that make him happy and content.

It's possible that you will not particularly want to have sex with your significant other, especially right after you come home from a business trip during which you just had a satisfying fling with someone else (for example, if you had sex in the morning and then caught a flight home and are now faced with more sex a few hours later). But find a way to get yourself stimulated, even if that means checking out some porn sites or fantasizing about another guy (try not to make it the one you just had sex with because…well, that's just gross).

You particularly need to show your man how much you missed him while you were out of town or away on business. If you express through your usual mannerisms that you want to have sex with him, this demonstrates to him that you probably behaved as you should have while you were gone and missed him terribly.

However, there is a trick to putting some extra time between sex with your fling and sex with your man. We all know what makes our spouse or companion tick, what puts him in a good mood and what destroys it. All it takes is that one intentional wrong word coming out of your mouth or some annoying behavior that would turn him off to spoil the sexual moment—then you're safe for another day. So as you are getting close to becoming intimate, intentionally say or do something to get him mad. Once he is upset, he will no longer be in the mood, and nothing will happen that night.

But tomorrow will be a different matter.

The important thing is for you to apologize to him the next day, mend all fences and try to be intimate with him as soon as possible. You will have bought yourself some time, removed any suspicions and saved his ego—possibly as well as your relationship.

Overall, the best way to not get caught is to keep up the appearance of normalcy. Save the freaky stuff for your flings!

Case Study #7

It had been three months since Samantha quit her last job and almost seven months since her last affair with a total stranger while on a business trip. As Sam is well aware, committing infidelity while away from home is the safest approach, and she has been quite successful with it during the past several years whenever the craving and desire to have sex outside her relationship overwhelmed her. She knew she had to do something since her life was getting too boring, not only in the normal routine but also in the bedroom.

In anticipation and preparation for an affair, she decided that a new and better Sam was needed to attract the type of man she was planning to have an affair with. To this end she decided to make some changes, such as going to the gym to get into better shape, receiving a complete body wax and buying a set of ultra-sexy underwear and some new, more-revealing clothing. Of course, she knew that she had to try them on her husband first to avert any suspicion.

One Friday afternoon, when her husband came home early, he discovered the new and improved Sam. The two had great sex; he appreciated the upgrade, and his ego went through the roof. When asked why she had made the improvement, Sam replied, "You deserve whatever I can do to make you happy because I love you very much."

She was convincing, and her husband was not complaining either. She kept up the appearance and upkeep for another five weeks when she decided it was time for real action. She called her friend Amanda in Wyoming and asked if she could come up to visit her for a few days. Amanda, a divorcee, welcomed her suggestion, and the two arranged for a three-day visit.

Sam prepared herself for the trip in the usual manner, using her checklist and her new attire since she was in the clear with her husband and his potential suspicion.

When she arrived, Amanda, a night nurse, picked her up at the airport, and the two headed to her home. Amanda apologized to Sam that she could not get the night off from work and hoped that Sam could entertain herself that evening, though she'd be off from work the remainder of her stay. Sam actually welcomed her predicament since she had never cheated in the presence of any known associate or friend; that, too, is part of The 9 Golden Rules (see next chapter).

As Amanda got ready for work, Sam prepared herself for a night out—after all, she was planning to get manhandled by a rough-and-tough cowboy. To dress for the part, she went to a local store, got herself some cowgirl gear and hit one of the local hangouts. She soon was noticed, and she reeled in a handsome and polite cowboy. The two spent the majority of the night together and, before dawn, she took a cab to Amanda's place.

The next couple of days she spent time with Amanda until the day of her flight back home. Sam insisted that she would take a cab to the airport and that Amanda should not concern herself with such a task. Sam had a plan—to see the cowboy one last time since her flight was not until 9:30 p.m.

The two met in the nearest hotel, and he rocked her world one more time for the road. As she was preparing for the airport, Sam went through her checklist per The 9 Golden Rules to ensure that everything was covered and nothing was left to chance.

She discarded the prepaid cell phone, extra condoms, cowgirl clothing and, of course, the panties she bought on the trip. It was now 5:45 p.m., and she had to take a shower and go to the airport. Her pre-trip preparation guidelines, all according to The 9 Golden Rules, taught her to pack unscented shampoo and body wash. Sam knew there would be only a few hours from the time she would shower to when her husband picked her up at the airport, so she had to be extremely careful and prepared.

On the plane, she decided that some intentional untidiness was required to mask her afternoon delight and the late shower, so when she arrived she did not turn her cell phone on. Instead, upon disembarking from the plane, she went to the restroom and removed and discarded her pantyhose. She then took her shoes off and walked quickly toward the baggage claim area. She needed the extra excursion to create additional sweat and mess up her hair a bit as only rushing would.

When she picked up her luggage, she turned her cell phone on and met her husband at the curb. The two went home and, upon arrival, she acted as if she were tired and needed to shower and clean up. Then she rewarded him for his trust as the two got intimate.

In contrast, Jennifer was divorced from her third husband and had had a boyfriend for the past fifteen months when, one day, her best friend, Anna, asked her to meet her at the new spa that had recently opened downtown. Anna had met a good-looking guy and, as this was their fifth date, she decided that tonight was his lucky night. In preparation, she made an appointment to get a Brazilian wax and encouraged Jen to do the same. At first, Jen was hesitant, but in the end she gave in.

Anna previously asked Jen to join her that evening since her date had an out-of-town friend visiting him. Jen agreed to do Anna the favor and make it a foursome.

Jen told her boyfriend that she was having a girls' night out with a few of her friends, something she had never done before. When asked who the friends were, Jen stumbled and mentioned some of her friends from high school, but the boyfriend had never heard of them before. With this lack of thoughtfulness and preparation, Jen was able to raise her boyfriend's suspicion and get on his radar.

Careless and unprepared, Jen went ahead and met Anna and her friends at 8:00 p.m. in a bar not too far away from her home. After pleasantries and small talk, Anna and her boyfriend disappeared and left Jen and the friend all alone to mingle.

Jen and her new male companion got along just fine, and after a few drinks they started kissing. Soon thereafter, they ended up in his hotel room. At around 1:30 a.m., she finally realized she had to head home. Fortunately, by that time, the boyfriend was already asleep, so any confrontation was averted.

But the next morning, as he got up to get ready for work, he found her clothes on the floor in the doorway and picked them up to place them on the chair. He smelled men's cologne and sniffed some more, finding the fragrance all over. He was going out of his mind and could not wait to wake her up to get some sort of explanation and find out what she had done the night before. Just then her cell phone started to vibrate.

What do you know? Up popped a picture of a half-naked guy with a caption that read, "It's the mailman." He had delivered and was damn proud of it, too! The young stud had saved his picture on Jen's phone so that it would appear each time he called. This was a childish gesture that caused Jen a huge headache right about then.

As the boyfriend tried to wake Jen up to no avail, he yanked the covers off of her and discovered her new Brazilian wax, which was too attractive to ignore. He put the whole puzzle together: high school friends he had never heard of, a full Brazilian, clothes that smelled of men's cologne and the phone call that put the nail in her coffin.

Jen had no way out of this situation other than admitting to the infidelity. The two broke up as a result of her lack of planning before having a fling.

So, as you can see, any time you women stray from your norm or lie unconvincingly, a red flag goes up, and you get on your man's radar. The questions he asks himself are, "Why the sudden change? What is she up to?" He looks for any other changes to put together more clues to prove your intention or lack of transparency. If you are in a committed relationship, sudden changes to your appearance and behavior are considered a method to attract unattainable partners, not the one you already have at home.

GOLDEN RULE

#8

Do Not Trust Your Best Friend

No offense, but women like to talk. (At least I think that's what they're doing when we're trying to watch the game.) That's why *Golden Rule #8* is short and, well, while not too sweet, at least it's to the point: do not tell anyone about your affairs. And that includes your best friend.

Who Can You Confide In?

The answer to that is simple. Two words: *no one*. Do not trust even your best friend with accounts of your infidelities—or anyone else for that matter (unless it's a paid professional, as you will read below). Never seek help from, share details with or admit to even your most trusted friend that you have committed adultery.

This may be extremely difficult, especially if the affair has left you feeling giddy and excited (as a successful fling should), but cheating on your significant other is a personal matter and should be one of your deepest secrets that you take with you to your grave. There is no trophy for or glory in cheating, and no one should envy you for such an act. Having an affair is something you do for yourself—and for you alone. It is intended for self-satisfaction and self-gratification; if you feel the need to brag about it, it means you didn't need an affair after all...what you need is an audience.

Imagine you have committed a crime. Would you share the details of it with anyone? Would you admit or confess to anyone? You must treat your affairs in a similar manner: conceal and deny them even if confronted by your best friend. While infidelity is not a crime (and can in fact be a "victimless" and harmless action but only if kept concealed), it can hurt you, your partner and a few other people if mishandled. That would be the real crime. So keep it to yourself and let your friends wonder about the "beauty secret" that has you glowing.

The rules in this book have trained and educated you to protect, empower and place yourself in a position of strength, authority and control when it comes to handling your affairs. Sharing the secret of your infidelity makes you weak, vulnerable and exposed and puts the situation completely out of your control. Quite frankly, talking about your fling puts you in more danger than actually acting on it in the proper way, and here are a few reasons why:

☞ Your best friend could share the news of your infidelity with her friends or your mutual friends.

☞ Your best friend may share the information with her husband or boyfriend, who is friends with your partner.

☞ Your best friend could share the details of your infidelity directly with your significant other out of guilt, compassion or an ulterior motive (like she's interested in him for herself, the little tramp!).

☞ Your best friend could turn around and blackmail you with the information—or at least hold it over your head.

☞ Women are notoriously bad at keeping secrets. Especially when wine is involved.

For all of the reasons above, you should consider discretion your new "best friend." Staying silent is the only way to stay in control.

Dear Diary, Dear Divorce Court

This may sound strange, but you also have to keep silent to yourself when it comes to your feelings about, reactions to and memories of your affairs. That doesn't mean you can't think or fantasize about it every now and then. But it does mean no journaling, scrapbooking, saving mementos or keeping a diary since all of these things can be discovered and used as evidence against you.

While it may seem cute or harmless at the time to keep a box of matches from the bar where you met your target, a small item from the hotel room or any scrap of paper with his handwriting on it, believe me, it won't seem that way once your significant other finds it. The same way you need to erase all incriminating texts and messages, you must get rid of all mementos.

Oh, and if you think your partner doesn't read your diary, think again. Using code words or initials to mask the other man's identity or to disguise your actions doesn't cut it. The only way to truly be safe is to keep the memory of the affair to yourself and not save souvenirs or commit a word to paper.

Of course, as much as it hurts me to say this, that also means discarding this book when you're finished reading it. After reviewing the contents in detail and taking notes as needed (keeping them in a desk drawer at work until you commit them to memory), you must get rid of this book since it is clear evidence of your intention to commit adultery.

When it comes to cheating, sex and sentimentality don't mix. Keep just the memories. Dump all the rest. Including the other man.

"Detail" Therapy

If you absolutely, positively have to tell someone about your indiscretions, consider a professional licensed therapist. For one thing, there is the safeguard of patient confidentiality. For another, your therapist is paid to listen (like a bartender but minus the booze).

Some women may just be bursting to tell someone all the details about their affairs, sort of like bragging or reliving the conquest. Some may want to unburden themselves of the guilt by opening up to another person, who stands in as a surrogate for the significant other. Others may want to find out just what it is that drives them to cheat in the first place. A therapist can fulfill any of these functions, and blabbing to a therapist is much safer than blabbing to your best friend.

By the way, if your therapist happens to be an attractive man, do not consider trying to kill two birds with one stone by making him a potential target; not only is it a bad idea, but it has "psychodrama TV movie of the week" written all over it. Avoid temptation: pick a female therapist or someone who looks like Dr. Phil.

In the end, keeping your affairs quiet takes discipline, will power and self-control—just like planning the affair in the first place. Having these attributes is a sign of maturity that means you're ready to embark on infidelity. Not having them means you're bound to get caught. So basically it comes down to this: if you can't keep your mouth closed, keep your legs closed.

Case Study #8

Jennifer was married to her fourth husband, Dave, and was enjoying a great life with this wonderful man and good provider. However, their sex life was not as satisfying as she anticipated and was accustomed to.

Jen was quite aware of her past tendencies and infidelities with multiple partners while she was in steady relationships, and for the first time she decided to do something about it to save her relationship. She went to a psychologist to assist her with her dilemma.

Jen hid this fact from Dave since she didn't want to hurt him or tell him the truth about her feelings, desires and what was lacking in their private life. It was apparent to the psychologist that his expertise was not best suited to Jen's situation, and he referred her to a sex therapist. To that end he selected an older female therapist from whom he had seen great results in treating his other patients. (This was for the best, since Jen felt an attraction to her psychologist.)

Jen started seeing the sex therapist for a few weeks when she noticed that, on Thursdays before her session began an attractive man would leave the therapist's office. She arranged her appointments so that the two could meet and get connected. Apparently, the sex therapy did not have an immediate impact since it usually takes years to see a positive and lasting result.

Regardless, the two saw each other every Thursday and began to exchange pleasantries and small talk; that soon worked its way to a coffee date in the nearby coffee shop. After a while, the attraction and desire were too powerful to overcome, so the two got intimate.

Meanwhile, a young couple moved next door to Jen and her husband. The neighbors, Cindy and Steve, were friendly and warm, and the two couples soon became good friends.

In time, the pressure and guilt of infidelity started to mount on Jen as the therapy began to have an impact on her. These feelings were new and strange, and she needed to vent them. So, one evening, as Jen and Cindy were having a glass of wine, Jen confided her indiscretions to her new neighbor in a moment of weakness. It was a dreadful mistake: Cindy shared this secret with her husband, Steve.

Weeks passed, and Jen's husband, Dave, wound up sharing with Steve the absence of sex in his life. Dave blamed himself for being too busy and involved with his business, but he also admitted that Jen had done little to encourage intimacy. As Dave began to more frequently complain about his sexual relationship with Jen, Steve decided not to conceal her infidelity any longer and revealed the truth.

So, the next Thursday, instead of following his usual schedule, Dave rented a car and parked across the street from the therapist's office to follow Jen's movements. An hour later he saw her leaving the medical building, followed by another car. Dave continued his pursuit and discovered his wife entering a motel parking lot with a white car right behind her.

He watched the two get out of their cars, kiss and hold hands before entering a room. He'd seen enough and headed home.

Since the two had signed a prenuptial agreement, Jen was out of his house, life and world within days—all because she let guilt get the better of her common sense and didn't follow **The 9 Golden Rules**.

Samantha, on the other hand, has never told a soul about her indiscretions...except me. And that was only after I promised to change her name for the purposes of this book!

GOLDEN RULE

#9

Deny Everything

This final chapter will highlight how to tell when your
significant other is catching on, what to do when the heat is
on and how to get the other man to move on. Okay, ladies,
read on.

Suspicious Minds

There are certain signs you need to look for that show that your man is getting suspicious. Some are obvious. If he starts inspecting your underwear with an infrared light, it's probably safe to say he's figured something out.

Some signs, however, are not as obvious. If he starts asking questions about where you're going and what you did—and he actually wants to hear all the details (most men would rather have a colonoscopy than listen to endless details about what you did all day)—or if he changes his schedule by staying home from poker night or volunteering to accompany you to the gym, chances are he's getting wise to what you're doing. At that point, to save the relationship and curtail further snooping, there's nothing for you to do but stay calm, stick to your story and end the affair or stop cheating until the heat is off.

Doing this, however, also takes preparation. You can't just suddenly quit the gym and stop working late at night; that would make him even more suspicious. Basically, the same prep work you did weeks in advance in order to start a fling should be applied when you're ready to end it or halt for a while until it's safe to resume. So once you stop the affair or one-night stands, maintain your same schedule and excuses for a while—except instead of sleeping with some guy, you should actually be doing what you *say* you're doing: working out and working late. Then you can gradually cut back on these activities and assume your normal, pre-affair life, and your significant other will be none the wiser.

If you're already planning to have another affair, wait long enough until your man's suspicion dies down...or at least until the start of football season, when his mind will be on other, more-important things.

What to Do if Your Man Finds Out

If the suspicion gives way to certainty and your significant other outright accuses you of cheating, there are three things you must remember: Deny. Deny. Deny. Unless he has hard proof or confronts you in the hotel lobby while you're with the other man—and even *those* situations are negotiable—you should *never* confess to infidelity.

After planning, quite possibly the second most important element in cheating successfully is the ability to deny an affair no matter the strength and amount of evidence collected against you by your spouse or partner. Your persistence in denying will eventually result in his acceptance of and belief in your innocence. If you're caught in a hotel lobby, for instance, you should deny that you and the other man ever had a room; instead, maintain that you just met your out-of-town client at his hotel restaurant for an early breakfast (or late dinner, depending on the time) because it was convenient. Make it seem like your significant other is crazy for even suspecting anything more. If he confronts you with photos taken by a private investigator, look at them casually and state, "I look nothing like this woman! Do you really think she's as pretty as me?" Turning the tables will make him feel cornered and flustered, taking the heat off of you.

There are many types of denial; however, for our purposes, we'll concentrate on denial of fact. Denial of fact is when someone avoids or obscures a fact by lying, which can take the form of an outright falsehood (commission), leaving out certain details in order to tailor a story (omission) or falsely agreeing to something.

Someone who is in denial of fact is typically using lies in order to avoid truths that they think may be potentially painful to themselves or to others.

The concept of denial is particularly important in infidelity because this kind of deception is used to lessen the harm and pain an adulterous affair might inflict on a spouse or companion by divulging the truth.

There are many reasons you should deny having an affair if you are caught by your husband or partner. There is your marriage or relationship, your life as you know it, your children and, finally, the financial repercussions. There is one more important reason, too, and that is the respect, honor and dignity of the man you love.

Rest assured that once you have been unfaithful, the agonizing truth will be intolerable and excruciating for your significant other. Denying it is the only medicine that could possibly relieve the pain. Although he might doubt your honesty and truthfulness, a bit of uncertainly could be all he needs to cling to in order to move forward and put the incident behind him. In that way, your lying is like throwing him a life raft so he doesn't drown in the knowledge that you cheated on him.

Even if you have found your soul mate through your affair and you want to end your relationship with your partner, it is not civilized to subject another human being to such cruelty by telling him the truth about your infidelity. You must act like a lady and remember that it is better to be deceitful and protect his dignity than to be honest and admit to the affair.

In contrast, if your fling is discovered by your significant other but you want more than anything to save your relationship, then the strategy is the same: lying and denying the affair is the only alternative. No matter how much he pushes you for the truth, do not give in. Deny, deny and deny some more until he eventually gives up.

When confronted in such a manner by your significant other, you must recognize that you will now be on his radar and must stop all affairs or infidelity for quite some time until his suspicion is gone. During this time period, try to be extra caring and loving and show a strong desire for sex with him (but not to the point of acting like a porn star, which will definitely raise some suspicion and red flags, among other things). Be persistent, and eventually he will forget all about his accusations because he *wants* to; in this particular scenario he doesn't *want* to be right. All he needs from you is to prove to (or at least minimally persuade) him that nothing happened, and he will be more than happy to accept it.

To be successful in cheating on your man and expecting to get away with it, you must be a good actress and a great pretender. By directly denying or masking the truth will be able to get out of any situation, especially if you are trapped by your significant other, who suspects you have been unfaithful. Some readers may argue that denying or masking the truth is the same as lying and that lying is not acceptable behavior in a relationship. But neither is cheating! And of the two, lying is definitely the less damaging to your relationship and his ego.

Denial is one of the most controversial defense mechanisms since it can easily be used to create an illusion of fact where the opposite is true. But the only way to deny and convince your man of this illusion is when you believe in it yourself. The best car salesmen believe so strongly in the product they are selling that they can convince anybody of buying that car.

After all, how can you convince your man you did not cheat on him unless you believe, through your own sense of denial, that you did not commit such an act? You should not judge yourself as an imposter or liar—simply as a woman who didn't really do anything wrong.

Denial, when combined with the power of persuasion, becomes an effective mechanism to convince even the most level-headed man that infidelity never took place. In most cases the result is successful because most men want to believe that their mates never cheated on them. A man's ego prohibits him from seeing and accepting this truth. So it is crucial to use your partner's

ego against him and persuade him that no one is better than he is and no one would ever be able to take his place in your heart, your life and—most important—your bed.

Do not attempt to buy his affections by showering him with gifts or insincere flattery. That is one mistake most amateurs make, so be sure to stay away from such confessional acts. Only a guilty woman attempts to mend her relationship with gifts or a sickly sweet attempt at innocence. Instead, simply deny any wrongdoing. Pretend the infidelity never took place and whatever he assumed was his imagination, not reality and not your problem!

After all, if you followed The 9 Golden Rules, no one other than you should ever know for certain your true identity or what you have done; therefore, your secret is safe and no one—not even someone who knows you as well as your man does— can contradict your story. As long as you stand strong.

The End of the Affair:
How to Act Like a Lady and Break It Off Like a Man

The whole point of this book is that cheating on your spouse or someone you love can be a harmless pastime and victimless crime—providing that you stick to the recommendations and follow The 9 Golden Rules. However, falling in love is another matter. For one thing, it means you didn't follow the rules, especially the one about "Never with the Same Man Twice," and you left yourself open to falling in love. In that case, it also means everyone involved stands to get hurt, which is the absolute worst-case scenario.

Let's suppose all the training and techniques discussed so far were not followed as recommended in this book. Somehow you got yourself into a situation in which you cheated on your significant other and now the other man has swept you off your feet, and all you can think about is being with him.

There are two possible explanations for your feelings:

☞ You found your soul mate.

☞ You are merely infatuated.

If he is truly, surely your soul mate—and we all have one—then you may have to follow your heart no matter what the consequences. Only very lucky people find their soul mates in their lifetime. If it is the other man and not your significant other, then you have to do what's best for you, not what's best for your current relationship.

Conversely, if the target of your fling is not your soul mate, then it is possible that you're just infatuated with him and that you have already found or married your true soul mate.

A mature woman should usually be able to tell the difference between the two scenarios. But sometimes infatuation hits hard and feels an awful lot like love. Time will often tell, but when you're already in a relationship, you don't have the luxury of time to continue a long-term affair while you figure out your feelings. In this case, before continuing the affair, consider the following questions and answer them as truthfully as you can:

☞ Can you imagine what it would be like to
  be unable to hold your significant other, kiss
  him, smell his scent or make love to him
  ever again?

☞ Can you imagine how ending the relationship
  will affect you, him, your jobs, your security

and your children (if you have any)?

☞ Can you calculate the financial and emotional costs of separation or divorce?

☞ Can you imagine what an outcast you will become among your friends and even family members?

☞ Can you imagine living life without your soul mate—and what if that turns out to be your significant other?

If you answered no to any of the above questions, then you know what you need to do. That good-looking fellow you may have met is not your soul mate and should be considered just a good memory. Treat it as such and nothing more. You should not talk about him or continue to think of him or the affair; remember, we call it a "one-night stand" for a reason. The strength to walk away from him and the affair is in you. You just need to recognize it—and act on it.

Think back to how it all started: first you planned an affair, then you worked out all the details, and then you proceeded to execute them. That's why the implementation of the plan is so critical to your success in cheating and getting away with it without harming yourself or others in the process.

All the important ingredients you've learned in this book are futile unless the plan to end the affair or one-night stand is put into motion with no exceptions or deviations. This is the last stage in the process. You must stop procrastinating; instead, have confidence in your strength and ability to execute and walk away.

In the world of adultery, emotion can't have any bearing on the decisions to be made because giving in to emotion will derail your ability to stay on course and follow your original plan. The profound impact that feelings can have on self-control and discipline could ultimately cause a lapse in judgment, which may result in discovery of your affair at this late stage in the game.

So how do you end the fling discreetly—and with no hard feelings or restraining orders? You must be polite but firm; leave no room for him to hope that the affair can continue... or for you to change your mind. Hopefully, you followed **The 9 Golden Rules** on this one and didn't use your true identity; therefore, he can't find you, hassle you or invade your private life and your world, which you worked so hard to protect. Your detailed plan will help you right about now; all you need is the discipline and will power to follow it, and everything will end as it should.

If you feel you are more like Jennifer than Samantha and do not have the necessary discipline and will power to set and stick to goals, then it is best for you to improve those skills before embarking on an affair. Otherwise, failure is a sure thing, and you'll probably end up hurting a lot of people on your way to your own destruction.

However, there is hope.

There are many exercise programs you can follow that will enhance your self-discipline and will power (we discussed a few in *Golden Rule #2*) when it comes time for pulling the trigger on your fling (not literally, of course; while it may seem like the easy solution, it's highly illegal—not to mention messy). These exercises will force you to do things you don't necessarily want to do, without letting emotion, procrastination or second thoughts stand in the way.

Here are a few additional exercises you can perform to enhance your abilities:

Exercise #1:

☞ Schedule a particular task in the morning
   and one in the evening.

☞ The tasks should not take more than
   ten minutes each and should be on the
   unpleasant side (such as cleaning the toilet).

☞ Start each task at its scheduled time.

☞ Do not alter the sequence of the tasks.

This exercise assists you in setting priorities that are based
on your needs and ultimate goal and not on any emotional
reactions or how you may feel at the moment.

Exercise #2:

☞ Spend an hour in the mornings and an hour
   in the evenings for one week to develop your
   personal and professional goals.

☞ Select these goals in different categories—
   for example, education, training, certification,
   investment opportunities, retirement plans,
   getting a promotion, toning up, etc.

☞ Do not develop details to accomplish any of
   the goals, just a general outline.

This exercise is considered progressive training, which
means as you succeed, you must gradually increase these
challenges to improve your self-discipline.

With improved self-discipline, you get into the habit of
setting goals and developing procedures (a plan) to accomplish

them. This is when you learn to plan your affair and set your desired goal, such as when, where, how and with whom.

Exercise #3:

☞ Select only one of the goals from Exercise #2.

☞ Spend two hours in the morning and two hours in the evening writing and developing details to accomplish this goal.

☞ The next day, spend the same amount of time reviewing and refining the steps you determine necessary.

☞ Develop timelines and finalize your plan.

This exercise helps you with organization and details for actual results. In this phase of the planning process, you learn to evaluate and detail your every move en route to your affair. For instance, when you're ready to end the affair, you should know exactly how and where you're going to do it and what exactly you're going to say. You should also rehearse responses to all of his potential reactions.

Exercise #4:

☞ Execute the plan. Start putting the steps into action.

☞ Follow through on the planned actions as precisely as detailed and without any alterations or deviations.

The advantage of this approach is that since the thought

process has already taken place, all risks have been evaluated and solutions developed, so you can proceed with confidence that you have done your utmost to succeed. No instant reactions or changes are allowed since you have considered all of the possible consequences of your actions before developing your course of action.

Remember: the important part of this process is that all these steps have taken place in the absence of emotion, so pure logic was used as the foundation for your decision-making. That won't be the case once the affair is underway.

Also be aware that it's a mistake to push yourself too hard when trying to build self-discipline; this is a gradual and time-consuming process. Do not try to transform your entire life overnight by setting dozens of new goals and expecting to accomplish them; using that strategy, you're almost destined to fail. Select easier exercises and then practice to improve and increase your inner strength and will power; this will translate into more self-confidence and success in everything you do— and that includes successfully starting and ending an affair.

The above exercises are effective methods for developing and improving your will power to perform certain tasks, actions and activities that you would rather avoid doing due to laziness, procrastination, weakness, emotional reactions, etc. But by performing such tasks you will overcome your subconscious resistance, train your mind to obey your will, strengthen your inner power and gain inner strength. Ending an affair is not necessarily an easy task, especially if you're enjoying it.

The 9 Golden Rules, collectively and individually, have been *selflessly* tested to produce the best possible results in terms of committing adultery and providing you with the necessary tools and training to conceal your act and to get away with it.

Of course, nothing in life is guaranteed, and **The 9 Golden Rules** are no exception. However, if followed and executed to perfection, they will substantially reduce your odds of getting caught with your pants down before you have a chance to pull them up again and end the affair with your ass covered.

Case Study #9

Jennifer had a short affair with one of her colleagues while she was in a serious relationship. The co-worker was married and was also well aware of Jen's status, so both were cautious. The two would meet at different hotels across town to avoid being seen together.

One night after their tryst at a hotel, Jen went home, took her clothes off and asked her boyfriend to take her coat to the cleaners the next day on his way to work. Jen was careless and didn't check her pockets as she should have before making such a request.

The next morning, when her significant other went through her coat pockets as a precaution, he discovered a shoehorn with a hotel logo; fortunately for Jen, the address and phone number were missing. He went upstairs and confronted her with the discovery. Jen had obviously made a few mistakes (having an affair with a co-worker, not showing attention to details), but if there was one thing she remembered from The 9 Golden Rules (and from her previous breakups), it was to deny the affair no matter how overwhelming the evidence against her might be.

To Jen's credit, she did not lose her nerves; she quickly came up with a story that the shoehorn belonged to one of her co-workers. She pointed to the new pair of heels she had worn and demonstrated to her boyfriend that they were still a little tight to put on and uncomfortable to wear.

At first he did not believe her, insisting that she had had an affair and vowing to get to the bottom of it. The more he drilled her with accusations and threats, the more Jen maintained her calm and repeated the same story over and over again. At one point she even encouraged him to contact the co-worker for verification of her claim.

Jen said, "I want you to come to work tomorrow and talk to Sarah yourself. I have nothing to hide, so there'll be no shame or embarrassment for me... maybe for you, though. In fact, I insist you do that because it's unfair for me to be accused of infidelity when I love you so much and would never do anything to ruin our relationship."

In the end, her seemingly sincere and passionate plea of innocence convinced her significant other that Jen was telling the truth. The potentially destructive storm passed without any harm, and I'm happy to say that Jen is still in that relationship— and is now an avid fan and follower of The 9 Golden Rules. It just cost her a few divorces and multiple breakups to finally join the club.

Compare that close call to Samantha's flawless execution of all The 9 Golden Rules. A couple of years ago, Sam went to Vegas for a two-day convention. She knew about it weeks in advance and had already begun preparation for a brief affair when her thoughts were logical and she wasn't caught up in a passionate moment.

After the first day there, she went to her hotel room, freshened up and went downstairs for dinner and some gambling. She met a man from Florida who was attending the same convention and introduced herself as Loni, a saleswoman from

Iowa (a place with which she was familiar from past business trips). Sam detected an opportunity to get intimate with this guy almost immediately since the attraction was certainly mutual.

She knew she had only one night since the next day they would both leave Vegas when the convention came to an end. Time was therefore of the essence. She had already used a false identity and contact information, and, according to plan, all other elements were in place for her to proceed with a possible fling with minimal risk of discovery or emotional attachment.

Knowing this one-night stand might linger well into the later hours of the next morning, and with the convention starting at 8:00 a.m. sharp, she managed to ask an associate from a different company to collect the necessary materials and notes so she could familiarize herself with the events that took place at the convention during her absence.

She spent the night with her new companion and, after a late breakfast ordered from room service, they parted ways with no promise of keeping in touch since they lived so far apart (she had chosen her target well).

Sam had approached the affair knowing that she had limited time to achieve her goal—which she accomplished in large part due to her advanced planning—and that it was not enough time to begin a full-blown affair. In other words, she knew she could easily walk away and that the salesman from Florida wouldn't be able to track her even if he wanted to.

Her entire business trip and affair can be divided into three planned sections:

☞ Pre-trip preparation

☞ On-trip preparation

☞ Return-home checklist

Pre-trip preparation

Before Sam embarked on this annual business trip, she purchased a prepaid cell phone and kept it at work for safekeeping. She did not share the phone number with anyone, especially her husband. The phone would be disposed of prior to her return home to eliminate the risk of contact from any individual she met on the trip.

Sam had purchased a software program and high-end business card papers so that, at her convenience at work, she could create identities with different names, phone numbers and addresses to suit her needs. She printed them and kept them with the cell phone in preparation for the trip. She then deleted the temporary computer files so no one could accidentally or purposefully discover her motivates and agenda.

She also had a list of different companies' convention attendees from previous years for contact purposes, and she casually phoned three of them to make sure that at least one would attend this year's convention. This was to ensure that she had coverage at the show in the event she was tied up with someone.

Prior to her departure, Sam went to the bank to obtain cash for her expenses to eliminate any trace of her activities while she was away from home.

On-trip preparation

When Sam arrived in Las Vegas, she immediately went to a nearby mall and purchased a new blouse and skirt. To conceal these purchases, she used the cash she had withdrawn from the bank prior to the trip. She also used cash for the extra hotel room she reserved—under a false name and using fake ID—to spend the night with her date. (Sam never uses the hotel room she booked for her trip since her husband is always aware of the name of the hotel, its phone number and her room number. Also, she tries not to go back to her target's room since she is less in control of the factors there.) Although this procedure costs more and can be cumbersome, it is necessary to reduce the risk of getting caught in the event that:

☞ Her husband calls the hotel room and the phone is answered by her date.

☞ Her husband drops in to catch her off-guard or surprise her.

Return-home checklist

Sam's return home was also planned out to the last detail. Before her departure, she went through her checklist to ensure she continued with her plan and did not leave anything to chance.

She discarded her new clothes and cell phone and made sure the convention manuals and handouts were available for viewing upon her return. She also purchased gifts for her kids but not for her husband, which was her usual habit and therefore wouldn't raise suspicion. She hid the souvenirs under the convention material when packing her carry-on bag, a subtle way to prove where she had been and what she did while away. The last thing Sam did before departure was to discard the checklist.

When she stepped on the plane, all evidence and thoughts of the affair were a distant memory. Although she'd be ready to deny whatever allegations of infidelity came her way, she never gave her husband any ammunition—thanks in large part to the teachings and guidelines of The 9 Golden Rules. And they lived happily ever after.

Conclusion

As you may already know (or imagine, or have fantasized about endlessly), cheating is a way to bring a little fun and excitement back into your life. In some case, it can recharge your sexual batteries and perhaps add some spice to your already existing, stable, monotonous—oops, I mean monogamous—relationship.

Some people even believe that the danger of getting caught adds an extra thrill, but that's like saying that the thrill of driving a fast sports car is somehow enhanced by the knowledge that the cops can pull you over at any minute, write you a ticket and add points to your record that will increase your insurance rates and possibly land you in driver's ed classes. Not very sexy, is it? Well, neither is a bad breakup.

The danger of getting caught needs to be removed (or reduced) from the equation in order for you to enjoy the affair unencumbered. Ironically, then, cheating is a little harmless fun only if you're serious about the endeavor and committed to putting some work and preparation into the careful planning and flawless execution of it. Otherwise, it can be a total disaster and mean the destruction of your relationship, not to mention your reputation, your loved one's feelings, your future and perhaps your life. All that for a little something on the side (well, hopefully not *too* little).

Luckily, you've got what all those celebrities, sports stars and politicians caught in sexual scandals didn't have. No, not just standards. Even better and more useful: **The 9 Golden Rules!**

Yes, they require preparation, planning and work. Yes, they call for discipline, self-control and will power. In those ways, they're just like taking yoga classes.

So if you're not up for the challenge, don't even consider cheating. You'll just end up straining something.

After reading this book, you should have a pretty good idea about the time, energy and effort it takes to cheat on your man and get away with it. For many women it's more than worth it. On the other hand, you may glance at your guy on the couch (I said "glance," not "scrutinize") and realize that your time, energy and effort may be better directed into what you already have—a fixer-upper. Or better yet, what you love about your current relationship is that it doesn't really require all that much energy and effort at all—a don't-even-bother.

Look—hopping into bed with another man is like hopping into a Ferrari. It may be fun, but it's not for everyone. Some will stay in control and have the time of their lives; those unable to handle the power and responsibility will ultimately crash and burn.

With **The 9 Golden Rules,** I've given you the keys to carrying on a successful affair. But you need to ask yourself one important question first: "Am I ready for the ride?"

The 9 Golden Rules "Cheat" Sheet

Golden Rule	Description
#1	Always plan ahead.
#2	Keep the "love" out of "love affair."
#3	Never cheat with someone you know.
#4	Hide the evidence.
#5	Get out of town.
#6	Cut the talk.
#7	Don't change your personal habits (*do* change your panties).
#8	Do not trust your best friend.
#9	Deny everything!

References

Power of Will, Frank C. Haddock (Pelton Publishing Company 1919)

"Denial," Wikipedia. The free encyclopedia

"Discipline," Wikipedia. The free encyclopedia

www.ingramcontent.com/pod-product-compliance
Lightning Source LLC
Chambersburg PA
CBHW071126280326
41935CB00010B/1133